Our Day Out

and other plays

is t

Willy Russell

Edited by David Self

STUDIO SCRIPTS

Stanley Thornes (Publishers) Ltd

First published in 1987 by Hutchinson Education
Reprinted 1988, 1989

Reprinted in 1991 by
Stanley Thornes (Publishers) Ltd
Ellenborough House
Wellington Street
CHELTENHAM GL50 1YD
England

Reprinted 1992 (twice)
Reprinted 1993 (four times)
Reprinted 1994 (twice)

British Library Cataloguing in Publication Data

Russell, Willy
    Our day out and other plays.—(Studio scripts).
    I. Title   II. Self, David   III. Series 822'.914
    PR6068.U86/

    ISBN 0 7487 1028 0

Printed and bound in Great Britain by SRP Ltd, Exeter

Contents

Introduction to the Plays

This anthology brings together four plays of proven popularity by Willy Russell, one of many creative artists produced in recent years by the city of Liverpool. Once a great port and thriving commercial centre, Liverpool has not had things easy over the last three decades with a brutal decline in trade and a tragic rise in unemployment. 'What's special about Liverpool?' goes a local joke. 'It's the city with no rush hour,' is the sick answer. This illustrates one of the distinctive characteristics of the Liverpudlian: no matter how grim life may seem, a native wit and sense of humour remains undefeated. That wit is present throughout these plays. Amusing though they are, however, they do not fail to tackle serious issues and to develop our sympathy for some of life's losers.

Our Day Out

Like another Liverpudlian dramatist, Alan Bleasdale, Willy Russell frequently writes about the people of his home city. This play chronicles a school outing: the Progress Class (i.e. a class for those with reading and writing problems) in an inner-city Liverpool school is being taken by coach on a day trip to Conwy in North Wales. In charge of the outing is the class teacher, the easy-going and motherly Mrs Kay – who, incidentally, is nobody's fool. However, fearing what may result from her tolerant attitudes, the Headmaster sends the very much stricter Mr Briggs along as well 'just to try and keep things in some sort of order'. Much of the play is taken up with the different reactions of these two teachers to the behaviour of the pupils at a roadside café, a zoo, at Conwy Castle itself and later on the beach.

Woven into what Briggs sees as a running battle between himself and Mrs Kay are a number of other story lines – for example, the relations between two younger teachers and the older boys and girls, and the problems of Carol, the girl to whom life offers so little in inner Liverpool that she is prepared not to go back. It is her threatened suicide that produces the climax of the day and almost brings about a change in Briggs's attitudes.

How Briggs will behave the day after the outing is just one of the many questions posed by Willy Russell's play, questions which will stimulate much discussion. Few of his characters are drawn in terms of black and white or good and evil. The moment one finds oneself 'siding' with a particular character or group of characters, they 'let you down', and the final reaction is that, while the play is frequently very funny, it is also an ultimately saddening picture of life as it is.

The realism of the play (as well as its humorous way of posing serious problems) was perhaps what caused it to be so well received when first shown on television. The *Daily Express* described it as a 'stunner', and 'a trip that shouldn't be missed': it is no wonder then that within six weeks of its first transmission it was repeated on BBC 1 as 'Play for Today'.

The Boy with the Transistor Radio

In this play, Willy Russell shows just how adept he is at

writing about people who lose out, despite their good intentions, and especially those trapped in the inner-city area of his native Liverpool. The tragic hero of this play is sixteen-year-old Terry. He is about to leave school and his father hopes to fix him up with a job in a local warehouse. Terry has little interest in this prospect. He lives in a dream world, created by a radio disc jockey who talks constantly of a great big wonderful world:

It's a beautiful day on 209, the sun's shining and everything's fine; England . . . you're beautiful – isn't she beautiful . . .? Yes. Good to have you along. I'm feeling good, you're feeling good which adds up to the fact that we're all feeling good . . . and that's good.

This leads Terry to dream of an idyllic future for himself in the sort of countryside which appears in television commercials for margarine and Hovis.

At school Terry's classmates talk of their job prospects but Terry has other ideas:

I'm getting a job with travel prospects and a car. An' when I grow up I'll have a wife who is dead smart with proper, nice kids and a house in the country and y'know . . . all that!

Terry believes all this will be made possible by the disc jockey, Float Jones, whom Terry has come to accept as a close personal friend. The teacher tries to show Terry the gap between his dream world and reality, but to no avail. Terry refuses to accept the truth because it is unbearably depressing; he even tries to demonstrate the reality of his friendship with Float by telephoning the disc jockey during a phone-in programme.

Eventually Terry does work in the warehouse but, in frustration and boredom, he vandalizes the loudspeaker through which the Float Jones programme is relayed to the workers. Given the sack, he attempts to find an escape by trying to teach himself the guitar.

This conflict between security and a desire to escape runs right through *The Boy with the Transistor Radio*. It is a compassionate yet painful play which explores the gulf between the dreams that are constantly dangled in front of us and the more mundane realities of everyday life.

Terraces

This television play could be set in any town that has a football team, but it is more than a play about football and its supporters.

The local team has just reached the cup final. For Danny, that is enough. He enjoyed watching the semi-final; he will (he hopes) enjoy the final. However, his neighbours and friends in the local pub want to make a public demonstration of their team loyalty. Eddy in particular is keen to show his excitement, and seizes on a chance remark of Danny's. They will paint all the houses in the street yellow (the team's colour) in order to publicize their support for the team. What is more, they hope it will attract media attention and bring film crews and television interviewers to the street. Danny refuses to follow suit and soon his is the only house not painted yellow. For him it is 'just stupid'. His wife Susan and son, Michael, try to persuade him to go along with the scheme – as do the others. 'You live in a community, Danny. You've got to think of others as well.' He maintains his independence, resisting the pressure 'to join the gang'. Eventually, after Susan's life has been made miserable and Michael has been picked on at school, Susan leaves Danny, taking Michael with her. Danny continues to try to maintain his freedom of choice and independence: what is merely awkwardness in the eyes of the others.

So is Danny a spoil-sport? Is he 'warped' as Susan

suggests? Or is he completely within his rights and noble in his refusal to conform, to follow the crowd? Like a good storyline from a well-written soap opera, *Terraces* raises many questions about the conflict between independence and what it means to be part of a close community.

I Read the News Today

Unlike the other plays in this collection, which were first written for television, *I Read the News Today* was commissioned by BBC School Radio.

It is about a teenager's sense of outrage that he is being manipulated; that the fashion and music that are being provided for him are synthetic, phoney and calculated. After venting his anger and frustration by destroying all the goods in a local warehouse, he has been taken to court and convicted. He has escaped from police custody and now (late at night) breaks into a local radio station. Wishing to broadcast his anger and bitterness about the way he has been exploited, he threatens the smooth-talking disc jockey with a gun. Eventually two (comic) policemen become aware that all is not well at the local radio station and the youth's attempt to explain his feelings to society are inevitably doomed.

A pertinent comment on 'the plastic society', the play is no mere 'discussion starter'. Nevertheless (like Willy Russell's other plays), it raises many topical and relevant discussion points, a few of which are outlined in the suggested 'Follow-up Activities' at the end of this book.

Willy Russell

Willy Russell was born in Whiston near Liverpool in 1947. His father worked in a factory before buying a chip shop. At school Willy was academically a failure which made his dream of becoming a writer seem impossible. On leaving school with one 'O' level English pass he became a ladies hairdresser. He soon determined, however, to leave the hairdressing trade and found a temporary job stacking boxes in a warehouse. Having returned to study at evening classes he then enrolled on a full-time 'A' level course, paying for it by cleaning on the night-shift at Fords. Whilst subsequently training as a teacher, Willy Russell wrote and produced his first stage play.

After 18 months of teaching and part-time writing, the success, in London, of his musical *John, Paul, George, Ringo and Bert*, enabled him to write full-time, resulting in many stage, television and screen plays, including *Stags and Hens, One for the Road, Educating Rita, One Summer* and *Shirley Valentine.*

Willy Russell's work has been produced and published extensively here and abroad. *Studio Scripts*, have also published his play *Lies* (City Life anthology) and *Blood Brothers* – which Willy subsequently transformed into a full-length musical. The success of his music has led to commissions to compose further scores for television and film.

Presenting the Scripts

The most informal classroom reading of a playscript is helped by rehearsal. Even a very experienced professional actor or actress prefers to look over his or her part before a first reading in front of colleagues. In the classroom, therefore, those who will be reading should be given time to look over their lines: to make sure that they know when to pause, when to 'interrupt' the previous speech, and to work out the changing mood of their character before they are asked to read aloud.

It is much easier to read to a group from the front of a traditional classroom, and from a standing position or a position where you can be seen by your audience. It may be helpful to appoint a 'director' who will decide the location of various settings and rehearse the actors in basic movements, checking that they know when and where to enter and exit.

Note that it is possible for a group to break into smaller groups, and for each of these to rehearse its own interpretation of one or more scenes, and then present their versions in turn to the whole class.

In preparing the scripts for inclusion in this book, some of the film and studio directions of the television plays have been slightly modified so that these directions (along with scene titles and descriptions of settings) can be read aloud by a narrator. In a classroom presentation, it might be helpful if he or she were in view of the 'audience' but away from the acting area.

Note that, provided these directions are read sympathetically, a television play (and certainly a radio play) will read as fluently in the classroom as will any other kind of play; but it should not be forgotten that the television plays were conceived in visual terms. It will therefore be fruitful to discuss (as the original director must have done) where and how each scene should be 'shot' to realize the author's intentions.

It will also be instructive to work out which scenes were recorded on a studio set, and for which scenes it was necessary to go filming on location.

Rehearsal and presentation (or even audio- or video-recording) of one of the shorter scripts (or of scenes from *Our Day Out*) could serve as a project for assessment in the Oral Communication domain of GCSE English or as a valid response to the text for assessment within an English Literature course.

Television plays on stage

A distinguishing feature of television plays is that, unlike stage plays, they can make speedy transitions from one scene to another. They can also include scenes which actually involve travel (for example, scenes where characters walk along a street or travel by bus).

The television scripts in this volume will work successfully on stage, however, if they are given a stylized production either in the round or on a proscenium stage. Specially-taken 35 millimetre slides, projected scenery or captions can announce locations to an audience, and the use of sound effects can be an effective substitute for detailed scenery (especially in, for example, the school scenes in *Our Day Out* and *The Boy with the Transistor*

Radio). Exterior scenes (such as the seaside scenes in *Our Day Out*) could be created by the use of slides, taped voices and sound effects. The use of stage furniture should be restricted so as to preserve fluency and speed of staging.

Costumes and hand-held props can also do much to replace scenery. In indoor scenes, the use of stage furniture should be restricted so as to preserve fluency and speed of staging. Part of the success of any television play lies in the fact that it can cut from one scene to another; and, in a stage performance of a television play, lighting changes must be used to effect such 'jump-cuts' and to make us believe the acting area now represents a different location.

Audio-recording

The following points may be of help when recording:
(a) Use your microphone to discover from how wide an angle it can pick up sound clearly.
(b) Even the best microphone cannot produce a good recording over a long distance from the sound source. For speech, it should be 30-40 centimetres from the mouth. (Those readers with stronger voices can obviously be further away than those who do not project so well.)
(c) It is much easier to record a play with actors standing rather than sitting. (They can easily tiptoe away when not involved in a dialogue, and so allow those who are speaking to stand in the best positions.)
(d) Do not hold the script between mouth and microphone, and avoid rustling pages.
(e) Rooms with bare walls produce a lot of echo. Unless an echo effect is required (for scenes set in a hospital

corridor, for example), if possible use a carpeted, curtained room for recording.

(f) Sound effects are important in any taped play. Don't worry about including every sound, but concentrate on those background noises which suggest location (for example, street noises, etc.) and sounds which indicate the arrival or departure of a character. Avoid clumsy and accidentally comic sounds (like artificial footsteps) which can clutter or confuse the much more important dialogue.

(g) Gently fading out the very last few words or sounds of a scene and fading in the first sounds of a new scene will suggest a transition from one scene to another.

A fairground scene from 'Our Day Out', first screened on BBC 2, 28 December 1977. © *BBC*

Our Day Out

First televised on BBC 2, 28 December 1977

Characters

The Teachers:
Mrs Kay (in her early forties)
Susan (early twenties)
Colin (early twenties)
Briggs (early thirties)
Headmaster

The Kids:

Carol (13)	**Andrews** (13)
Reilly (15)	**Ronson** (13)
Digga (15)	**Kevin** (12)
Linda (15)	**Jimmy** (12)
Karen (15)	**Maurice** (12)

Other kids (all around 12 or 13)

Other Adults:

Les, the 'lollipop man'	**John**
The Driver	**Mac**
Mrs Roberts	**Animal Keeper**
Waitress	**Two other Animal Keepers**

Our Day Out

---

1   In the street

The street is in the inner city of Liverpool. **Kids** *are streaming in one direction. It is approaching 9 a.m. The* **kids** *are pushing, shoving, rushing, ambling, leering and jeering. A group of older kids cross the road, ignoring the lollipop man's assistance. He points them out to a passing woman, obviously disgusted.* **Carol** *rushes along the street wearing a school uniform which doubles as a street outfit and her Sunday best. She is eating half a sandwich and clutching a supermarket carrier bag. She arrives at the road-side and, as there isn't a vehicle in sight, goes to cross without bothering to enlist the aid of the lollipop man,* **Les.** *He stops her from stepping off the pavement.*

Les: 'Ey you!

Carol: [*Stopping*] What?

Les: Come here. Come on!

Carol: [*Approaching him*] Agh ey, Les. Come on. I wanna get t' school.

Les: That makes a bloody change.

Carol: We're goin' out. On a trip.

Les: Now listen. Are you listenin'? Y' don't cross the road without the assistance of the lollipop man. And that's me!

Carol: There's nott'n comin', though.

Les: Now just you listen; I know it might look as though there's nothin' comin' but how do you know that a truck or car isn't gonna come speedin' out of that side road? Eh?

Carol: [*Looking*] Oh yeh. I never thought of that.

Les: No. I know y' didn't. Y' never do. None of y'. That's why the government hired me to look after y' all.

Carol: Ta Les.

Les: Ey. Where y' goin' today then?

Carol: It's somewhere far away. I forget.

Les: They all goin'?

Carol: Only the kids who go the Progress Class.

Les: What's that?

Carol: What? Y'don't know what the Progress Class is? It's Mrs Kay's class. Y' go down there in the week if y' can't do sums or writing. If y' backward like.

Les: By Christ, I'll bet she's kept busy. They're all bloody backward round here.

Carol: I know. Come on Les. I wanna get there.

[**Les** *looks up and down the road. Not a vehicle in sight*]

Les: Just hold it there.

Carol: There's nott'n comin'.

[**Les** *looks down the road. In the distance a car is just appearing*]

Carol: Oh come on, Les.

[**Les** *holds out his arm to prevent her from crossing. Only when the car is within striking distance does he walk out with his 'Stop' sign. The car pulls to a halt.* **Les** *waves* **Carol** *across*]

Les: [*Quietly to* **Carol** *as she passes*] I got him that time. Arrogant get that one is.

[**Carol** *continues on her way. The driver of the car glares as* **Les** *waves him on*]

2   The school gates

A coach. Various groups of **Kids** *are scattered near by. One group surrounds a teacher,* **Mrs Kay**, *all of them after her attention. Cries of, 'Miss, miss, miss, me mum said I could go, miss,' and 'Miss, can I come if I haven't got enough money?' and, 'Miss, can I come, miss?'*

Mrs Kay: All right, all right. Will you just let me have a minute's peace and I'll get you all sorted out. Right. Now those who've got permission to come on the trip but haven't yet paid, I want you to come over here.

[*She moves a short distance away and all the kids follow her.* **Briggs** *surveys this scene*]

Mrs Kay: [*Bright*] Good morning, Mr Briggs.

Briggs: [*Begrudged*] Morning.

[*He turns and enters the school*]

Briggs: [*To a couple of boys*] Come on, move!

3   The Headmaster's office

The **Headmaster** *is talking to* **Briggs**, *who was the driver of the car.*

Headmaster: Well I'd like you to go with her, John. We can get Frank Collins to take over your examination classes for the day. I'd just like you to be there and keep an eye on things. I don't want to be unprofessional and talk about a member of staff but I get the impression she sees education as one long game.

Briggs: Well . . . if the antics in her department are anything to go by. . . ! She always reminds me of a mother hen rather than a teacher. . . .

Headmaster: Well, anyway, just try and keep things in some sort of order.

4   The school gates

Mrs Kay *is talking to two young teachers,* **Colin** *and* **Susan.** *Around them are excited, lively kids – not lined up but in random groups.*

Mrs Kay: [*Shouting to a* **Kid**] Maurice! Come away from that road will you?

[*The* **Kid** *does so. Two older* **Kids** *come rushing out of school and up to the* **Teachers**]

Reilly: Miss . . . miss, can we come wit' y'? Can we?

Mrs Kay: Oh, Brian! You know it's a trip for the Progress Class.

Reilly: Agh, ay, miss, we used t' be in the Progress Class though.

Susan: But you're not now, Brian. Now you can read and write you're back in normal classes.

Mrs Kay: Look Brian. You know I'd take you. But it's not up to me. Who's your form teacher?

Reilly: Briggsy.

Mrs Kay: Well, you'll have to go and get his permission.

Reilly: [*As he and* **Digga** *rush off*] You're ace, miss.

Mrs Kay: Brian!

[*He stops*]

Bring a note.

Reilly: [*Worried*] Ah . . . what for, miss?

Mrs Kay: [*Smiling*] Because I wasn't born yesterday, Brian Reilly, and if I don't ask you for a note you'll just hide behind the corner for ten minutes and say he said you could go.

Reilly: [*Knowing she's got him sussed*] As if we'd do a thing like that, miss!

Carol: [*Tugging at Mrs Kay's arm*] Where are we goin', miss?

Mrs Kay: Carol . . . Miss Duncan's just told you. Conwy. We're going to Conwy.

Carol: Miss is that in England, eh?

Colin: It's in Wales, Carol.

Carol: Will we have t' get a boat?

Mrs Kay: Carol . . . we're going on a coach. Look, it's there. You can get on now.

[*She shouts out to the rest of the* **Kids**]

Go on . . . you can all get on now.

[*There is a wild rush of* **Kids** *to the coach doors. The* **Driver** *appears and blocks the way*]

Driver: Right. Just stop there. Don't move.

Kid: Miss said we could get on.

Driver: Oh, did she now?

Kids: Yeh.

Driver: Well, let me tell youse lot something now. Miss isn't the driver of this coach. I am. An' if I say y' don't get on, y' don't get on.

Mrs Kay: Is anything wrong, Driver?

Driver: Are these children in your charge, madam?

Mrs Kay: Yes.

Driver: Well y' haven't checked them, have y'?

Mrs Kay: Checked them? Checked them for what?

Driver: Chocolate an' lemonade! We don't allow it. I've seen it on other coaches madam; fifty-two vomitin' kids . . . it's no joke. No, I'm sorry, we don't allow that.

Mrs Kay: [*To* **Susan**] Here comes Mr Happiness. All right, Driver . . . I'll check for you.

[*To* **Kids**]

. . . Now listen, everyone. If anybody's got any chocolate or lemonade I want you to put your hands up.

[*A sea of dumb faces and unraised hands.* **Mrs Kay** *smiles at the* **Driver**]

There you are, Driver. All right?

Driver: No, it's not all right. Y' can't just take their word for it. They have to be searched. Y' can't just believe kids.

[*Pause.* **Mrs Kay** *stares at him. She could blow up but she doesn't*]

Mrs Kay: Can I have a word with you, Driver, in private?

[*Reluctantly the* **Driver** *gets off the coach and goes across to her. She manoeuvres it so that he has his back to the coach and the* **Kids**]

What's your name, Driver?

Driver: Me name? I don't usually have to give me name.

Mrs Kay: Oh, come on . . . what's your name?

Driver: Suttcliffe, Ronny Suttcliffe.

Mrs Kay: Well, Ronny, [*Pointing*] take a look up these streets. [*He does and she motions the other teachers to be getting the* **Kids** *on the coach*] Ronny, would you say they were the sort of streets that housed prosperous parents?

Driver: We usually only do the better schools.

Mrs Kay: All right, you don't like these kids. I can tell that. But do you have to cause them so much pain?

Driver: [*Shocked*] What have I done? I only told 'em to wait. . . .

Mrs Kay: Ronny, the kids with me today don't know what it is to *look* at a bar of chocolate. Lemonade never touches their lips. [*We almost hear the violins*] These are the children, Ronny, who stand outside shop windows in the pouring rain, looking and longing and never getting. Even at Christmas, at Christmas-time when your kids from the better schools are opening presents and singing carols, these kids are left to wander the cold cruel streets.

[*Pause as she sees the effect she is having. The* **Driver** *is grief-stricken*]

5   Inside the coach

The kids are stuffing themselves with sweets and lemonade. The **Driver** *comes on board and by the time he turns to face the* **Kids** *there is not a bottle of lemonade or chocolate bar in sight. The* **Driver** *puts his hand into his pocket and pulls out a note.*

Driver: Here you are, son, [*To* **Kid** *in front seat*] run over to the shops an' get what sweets y' can with that.

[*The* **Kid** *takes the money and gets off the coach.* **Susan,** *the young teacher, leans across to* **Mrs Kay**]

Susan: What did you do?

Mrs Kay: Lied like hell, of course!

[*She gets up and faces the kids*]

Now, will you listen everyone. We'll be setting off for Conwy in a couple of minutes.

[*Cheers*]

Now listen! We want everyone to enjoy themselves, so let's have no silly squabbling or doing anything that might be dangerous to yourselves or to others. That's the only rule we have today: think of yourselves, but think of others as well.

[**Reilly** *and* **Digga** *rush into the bus*]

Reilly: Miss, miss, we're comin' wit' y', miss. He said it's all right.

Mrs Kay: Brian, where's the note?

Reilly: He didn't give us one, miss. He's comin' himself. He said to wait.

[**Digga** and **Reilly** *go to the back of the coach.* **Mrs Kay** *looks at* **Colin** *and* **Susan**]

Colin: He's coming to keep an eye on us.

Susan: Make sure we don't enjoy ourselves.

Mrs Kay: Ah well. We'll just have to deal with him the best way we can.

[*She sits down next to* **Carol**. *On the back seat of the coach* **Reilly** *and* **Digga** *are facing some small kids*]

Reilly: Right, dickheads. Move!

Little Kid: Why?

Reilly: Cos we claimed the back seat, that's why.

Little Kid: You're not even in the Progress though.

Digga: We used to be though, so move.

Reilly: Yeh. Respect y' elders!

[*At the front of the coach,* **Briggs** *is climbing aboard. He stands at the front and stares and glares. The* **Kids** *sigh – he is a cloud on the blue horizon*]

Briggs: [*Suddenly barks*] Reilly. Dickson. Sit down!

Reilly: Sir, we was only. . . .

Briggs: [*Staccato*] Sit down, now, come on, move!

[**Reilly** *and* **Digga** *sit on the two small kids who move to make room for them*]

Briggs: Go on, sort yourselves out!

[*He leans across to* **Mrs Kay** *and speaks quietly*]

You've got some real bright sparks here, Mrs Kay. A right bunch.

Mrs Kay: Well, I think we'll be safe now that you've come to look after us.

Briggs: [*Looking at the* **Kids**] There's a few of 'em I could sling off right now.

Mrs Kay: Oh, you are coming with us then?

Briggs: The Boss thought it might be a good idea if you had an extra member of staff.

[*Stands to address the* **Kids**]

Right, listen.

[*Pause*]

We don't want you to think that we don't want you to enjoy yourselves today, because we do! But a lot of you haven't been on a school visit before so you won't know *how* to enjoy yourselves. So I'll tell you. To enjoy a coach trip we sit in our seats. We don't wander up and down the aisle. We talk quietly to our neighbour, not shout at our mates four seats down.

[*Staccato*] Are you listening, girl! We look nicely out of the windows at the scenery. And we don't do anything else.

[*Throughout the speech the* **Kids** *look disappointed*]

Don't worry, I've driven in my car behind school coaches and seen it. A mass of little hands raised in two-fingered gestures to the passing cars. Yes. But we won't do that will we? Will we?

[*Chorus of:* 'No, sir.']

Briggs: No, sir. We won't.

[*The* **Kid** *returning from the shop, armed with sweets, climbs onto the bus*]

Kid: I've got them . . . I've got loads. . . .

Briggs: Where've you been?

Kid: Gettin' sweets, sir.

Briggs: Sweets?

Mrs Kay: [*Reaching for sweets*] Thank you, Maurice.

Briggs: Sweets?

[*The* **Driver** *taps* **Briggs** *on the shoulder*]

Driver: Excuse me, can I have a word with you, please?

Briggs: [*Puzzled*] Yes.

[*The* **Driver** *gets off the coach and* **Briggs** *follows.* **Mrs Kay** *gives the sweets to* **Susan** *who starts to dish them out. We hear a snatch of the* **Driver's** *speech to* **Briggs**]

Driver: The thing is, about these kids, they're like little souls lost an' wanderin' the cruel heartless streets. . . .

[*Inside the coach,* **Colin** *has joined* **Susan** *in giving out the sweets.* **Colin** *is at the back seat*]

Reilly: How y' gettin' on with miss, eh sir?

Digga: We saw y', sir, goin' into that pub with her, sir.

[**Susan** *is watching in the background*]

Colin: [*Covering his embarrassment*] Did you?

Reilly: Are you in love with her, sir? Are y'?

Colin: [*Making his escape*] All right . . . you've all got sweets have you?

Reilly: Sir's in love, sir's in love!

[**Reilly** *laughs and jeers as* **Colin** *makes his way down the aisle*]

Susan: Watch it, Brian!

Reilly: [*Feigned innocence*] What?

Susan: You know what.

Reilly: Agh ey, he is in love with y' though, isn't he, miss.

Digga: Miss, I'll bet he wants t' marry y'.

Reilly: You'd be better off with me, miss. I'm better lookin'. An' I'm sexier!

Susan: [*Giving up playing it straight. She goes up to him, leans across and whispers*] Brian . . . little boys shouldn't try to act like mén. The day might come when their words are put to the test!

[*She walks away*]

Reilly: [*Jeering*] Any day, miss . . . any day . . . [*Laughs*]

Digga: What did she say? What did she say?

Reilly: Said she fancied me.

[*At the front of the coach,* **Briggs** *and the* **Driver** *are climbing back on board.* **Briggs** *sits opposite* **Mrs Kay**. *He leans across to her*]

Briggs: [*Quietly*] We've got a right head case of a driver.

[*The engine roars into life. The* **Kids** *cheer.* **Briggs** *turns round with a warning look as the coach pulls away from the school. Thousands of little fingers raise in a V-sign out of the windows*]

6   Leaving the city

As the coach goes along the city streets the **Kids** *are talking and laughing and pointing. On the back seat,* **Reilly** *secretly takes out a packet of cigarettes. The* **Little Kid** *sees them.*

Digga: Reilly, light up.

Reilly: Where's Briggsy?

Digga: He's at the front, I'll keep dixie. Come on, we're all right, light up.

Little Kid: Agh 'ey. You've got ciggies. I'm gonna tell miss.

Reilly: Shut up you an' open that friggin' window.

Little Kid: No . . . I'm gonna tell miss.

Digga: Go'n tell her. She won't do nott'n anyway.

Kid: I'll tell sir.

Reilly: You do an' I'll gob y'.

Digga: Come on . . . open that window, you.

Kid: Why?

Reilly: Why d' y' think? So we get a bit of fresh air.

Kid: Well there's no fresh air round here. You just wanna smoke. An' smokin' stunts y' growth.

Reilly: I'll stunt your friggin' growth if y' don't get it open.

[**Andrews** *gets up and reaches for the window*]

Andrews: I'll open it for y' Reilly.

[**Reilly** *ducks behind the seat and lights up*]

Andrews: Gis a ciggy.

Reilly: Get y' own ciggies.

Andrews: Ah go on. I opened the window for y'.

Digga: Y' can buy one off us.

Andrews: I can't. I haven't got any money.

Reilly: Course y've got money.

Andrews: Me ma wouldn't give me any. She didn't have any.

Digga: Go 'way . . . your ma's loaded.

Andrews: No she's not.

Reilly: Well she should be . . . all the fellers she picks up on Parly.

Andrews: Go on . . . gis a ciggy.

Digga: She's always with the blacks off the boats, your ma. And they're loaded, them blacks are.

Reilly: An you must have money cos they pay a fortune for a bit of White.

Andrews: Well *I've* got no money . . . honest.

Digga: Well, y've got no ciggies either.

Andrews: I'll give y' half me sarnies for one ciggie.

Reilly: What's on 'em?

Andrews: Jam.

Reilly: I hate jam.

[*They have become lax about keeping an eye out and do not notice* **Briggs** *getting up from his seat and approaching the back of the coach.* **Digga** *suddenly looks up and sees him*]

Digga: Briggs!

[**Reilly** *passes the cigarette to* **Andrews**]

Reilly: Here!

Andrews: Ta.

[**Andrews** *takes it and, making sure that his head is out of sight, he takes a huge drag. When he looks up,* **Briggs** *is peering down at him*]

Briggs: Put it out!

Andrews: Sir, sir, I wasn't. . . .

Briggs: Put it out. Now get to the front of the coach.

Andrews: Sir, I was just. . . .

Briggs: I said get to the front!

[**Andrews** *sighs, gets up and goes to the front of the coach.* **Briggs** *sits in* **Andrew's** *seat*]

Briggs: Was it your ciggie, Reilly?

Reilly: Sir, I swear on me mother.

Digga: Don't believe him, sir. How can he swear on his mother. She's been dead for ten years.

Briggs: All right, all right. We don't want any argument. There'll be no more smoking if I stay up here, will there?

[**Carol**, *who is sitting next to* **Mrs Kay**, *is staring out of the window*]

Carol: Isn't it horrible, eh, miss.

Mrs Kay: Mm?

Carol: Y' know . . . all the thingy like. The dirt an' that.
[*Pause*] I like them nice places.

Mrs Kay: Which places?

Carol: Y' know them places on the telly. Where they have gardens an' trees outside an' that.

Mrs Kay: You've got trees in Pilot Street, haven't you?

Carol: We did have till last bommy night – the kids chopped 'em all down an' burnt them all. [*Pause*] Miss, y' know when I grow up, miss. Y' know if I started to work hard now an' learned how to read, eh? Well, d' y' think I'd be able t' live in one of them nice places?

[*Pause*]

Mrs Kay: Well you could try, couldn't you, love. Eh?

Carol: Yeh.

[**Mrs Kay** *smiles at her and links her arm. At the back, the kids are all stifled and bored by* **Briggs's** *presence*]

Briggs: [*Pointing out of the window at the South Docks*] Now just look at that over there.

[**Digga** *looks but sees nothing*]

Digga: What?

Briggs: What? Can't y' see? Look, those buildings. Don't you ever bother looking at what's around you?

Reilly: It's only the docks, sir.

Briggs: You don't get buildings like that anymore. Just look at the work that must have gone into that.

Reilly: D' you like it down here, sir?

Briggs: I'm often down here at weekends, taking notes, photographs. [*Sharply*] Are you listening, Reilly? There's a wealth of history that won't be here much longer.

Reilly: Me old man works down here, sir.

Briggs: What does he think about it?

Reilly: He hates it.

Briggs: His job or the place?

Reilly: The whole lot.

Briggs: Well, you tell him to stop and have a look at what's around him. Yes, he might see things a bit differently then.

[**Briggs** *looks up and sees* **Linda** *kneeling up on her seat and talking to the girl behind her*]

Karen: Wales is cracker.

Briggs: Linda Croxley!

Linda: [*Not even looking up*] What?

[**Briggs** *gets up and goes across to her. She waits until the last possible moment before sitting 'properly' in her seat*]

Briggs: What sort of outfit's that for a school visit?

[*She is dressed in the prevailing pop outfit of the day*]

Linda: [*Chewing. Contemptuous. Looking out of window*] What!

Briggs: Don't you 'what' me young lady.

[*She shrugs*]

You know very well that on school visits you wear school uniform.

Linda: Well. Mrs Kay never said nott'n about it.

Briggs: You're not talking to Mrs Kay.

Linda: Yeh. I know.

[*Pause*]

Briggs: [*Leaning in close. Threatening*] Now listen here young lady — I don't like your attitude one bit!

Linda: What have I said? I haven't said nott'n yet, have I?

Briggs: I'm talking about your attitude. [*Pause*] I'm telling you now. Carry on like this and you'll be spending your time in Conwy inside this coach.

Linda: I don't care. I don't wanna see no crappy castle anyway.

Briggs: [*Pointing*] Count yourself lucky you're not a lad. [*Pause*] Now I'm warning you, Miss Croxley, cause any more unpleasantness on this trip and I'll see to it that it's the last you ever go on. [*Pause*] Is that understood? Is it?

Linda: [*Still looking out of window*] Yes. [*Sighs*]

Briggs: It better had be.

[*He makes his way down to the front of the coach and takes his seat next to* **Andrews.** *Across the aisle* **Briggs** *sees that* **Mrs Kay** *has taken off her shoes and has her stockinged feet curled up under her.* **Carol** *has her arm linked through* **Mrs Kay**'s *and is snuggled up to her – they look more like mother and daughter than teacher and pupil. Behind* **Briggs,** **Linda** *is kneeling up again,* **Reilly** *and company have started smoking and there are lots of kids eating sweets, drinking lemonade and larking about. He addresses the kid next to* **Andrews**]

Briggs: Right, what's your name?

[*Pause*]

Briggs: Wake up!

Maurice: Sir, me!

Briggs: What's your name?

Maurice: McNally, sir.

Briggs: Right, McNally, go and sit at the back.

Maurice: Sir, what for?

Briggs: Never mind what for, just do what you're told, lad.

[**Maurice** *goes to the back of the coach*]

Briggs: [*To* **Andrews**] Right, move up! How long have you been smoking, Andrews?

Andrews: Sir, I don't smoke.

[*Pause as* **Briggs** *looks at him*]

Sir, since I was eight, sir.

Briggs: And how old are you now?

Andrews: Sir, thirteen, sir.

Briggs: What do your parents say about it?

Andrews: Sir, sir, me mum says nott'n about it but when me dad comes home, sir, sir, he belts me.

Briggs: Because you smoke?

Andrews: Sir, no sir, because I won't give him one.

[*Pause*]

Briggs: Your father goes to sea does he?

Andrews: What? No, sir.

Briggs: You said 'when he comes home', I thought you meant he was away a lot.

Andrews: He is, sir, but he doesn't go to sea.

Briggs: What does he do?

Andrews: I dunno, sir, sir, he just comes round every now an' then an' has a barney with me mam. Then he goes off again. I think he tries to get money off her but she won't give him it though. She hates him. We all hate him.

[*Pause*]

Briggs: Listen. Why don't you promise yourself that you'll give up smoking. You must realize it's bad for your health.

Andrews: Sir, I do, sir. I've got a terrible cough.

Briggs: Well, why don't you pack it in?

Andrews: Sir, sir, I can't.

Briggs: Thirteen and you can't stop smoking!

Andrews: No, sir.

Briggs: [*Sighing, shaking his head*] Well you'd better not let me catch you again.

Andrews: No, sir, I won't.

[*Pause as they each go into their respective thoughts.* **Briggs** *turns and looks at* **Mrs Kay**. *She looks at him and smiles warmly. He tries to respond but doesn't quite make it.* **Colin** *walks along the aisle generally checking that everything is all right. As he gets near* **Linda's** *seat her friend,* **Karen**, *taps her and points him out.* **Linda** *immediately turns round and smiles at* **Colin**. *It's obvious that she fancies him*]

Linda: Sir, y' comin' to sit by me are y'?

Karen: [*On the seat behind* **Linda**] Don't sit by her, sir . . . come an' sit by me.

Colin: I've got a seat at the front, thanks.

Linda: 'Ey, sir.

Colin: What, Linda?

Linda: Come here, I wanna tell y' somethin'.

Colin: Well, go on.

Linda: Ah ey sir, I don't want everyone to hear. Come on, just sit down here while I tell y'.

Karen: Go on, sir . . . she won't harm y'.

Linda: Come on, sir.

[*Reluctantly* **Colin** *sits by her.* **Karen's** *head is poking through the space between the seats and both girls laugh*]

Colin: What is it?

[*They laugh*]

You're not goin' to tell me a joke, are you?

[*The girls laugh even more*]

Well, I'll have to go.

[**Linda** *quickly links her arm through his and holds him there*]

Linda: No, sir ... listen. Listen, she said, I wouldn't tell y' ... but I will. [*Pause*] Sir, I think you're lovely.

Colin: [*Quickly getting up. Embarrassed*] Linda!

[*He walks away from the girls to the back of the coach*]

Linda: I told him. I said I would. Ooh ... he's ace isn't he?

Karen: You've got no chance. He's goin' with miss.

Linda: I know. [*Pause*] He might chuck her though an' start goin' with me. He might marry me.

Karen: [*Shrieking*] Ooer! Don't be stupid, you. You won't get a husband like sir. You'll end up marryin' someone like your old feller.

Linda: You're just jealous you, girl.

Karen: Get lost.

[**Colin** *talks to the lads on the back seat.* **Reilly** *hides a cigarette in his cupped hand*]

Colin: All right lads ... it shouldn't be too long before we're getting into Wales.

Little Kid: That's in the country, Wales, isn't it, sir?

Colin: A lot of it is countryside, yes.

Reilly: Lots of woods, eh sir?

Colin: Woods and mountains, lakes ...

Reilly: You gonna take miss into the woods, are y', sir?

Colin: [*Pause*] Now just watch it, Brian, all right?

Reilly: Sir, I just meant was y' gonna show her the trees an' the plants. . . .

Colin: I know quite well what you meant.

[*Turns to go*]

And if I was you I'd put that fag out before you burn your hand. If Mr Briggs sees that you'll be spending the rest of the day alongside him. Now come on, put it out.

[**Reilly** *takes a last mammoth drag and then stubs out the cigarette.* **Colin** *walks back along the aisle*]

Reilly: [*Shouting after him*] I'll show her the woods for y', sir.

[**Colin** *pretends not to hear.* **Reilly** *leans across to the* **Little Kid** *in the seat in front and knocks him*]

Reilly: Give us a sweet you, greedy guts.

Kid: I've only got a few left.

Digga: You've got loads.

Kid: I haven't.

Reilly: Let's have a look then.

[*The* **Kid** *falls for it and shows him the bag.* **Reilly** *snatches it*] Ta!

7   In the country

The coach is on a country road. **Mrs Kay** *is talking to the* **Driver.**

Mrs Kay: Ronny, I was just wondering, is there somewhere round here we could stop and let the kids stretch their legs a bit?

Driver: Well I'll tell y' what, Mrs Kay, there's a few cafés a bit further on. D' y' want me to pull into one of them?

Mrs Kay: Smashing.

8   A roadside café

Outside the café there are signs saying: 'Open' and 'Coaches Welcome'. Inside the café, a **Waitress** *is working on the tables. There is also a woman,* **Mrs Roberts,** *working behind the counter.*

Waitress: [*Looking up and seeing coach in distance*] Better be getting some cups ready, Mrs Roberts. There's a coach comin'.

Mrs Roberts: [*Moving over to window*] Where is it?

Waitress: Probably pensioners so early in the season.

Mrs Roberts: [*Worried*] No. I don't . . . I don't think so.

   [*She moves behind the counter and produces a pair of binoculars*]

   Let me see.

   [*She lifts the binoculars and looks at the coach. She can see the kids and the destination indicator which reads: 'Liverpool to Conwy'. She lowers the binoculars and frowns a worried frown*]

   Right! Come on, action!

9   Inside the coach

Mr Briggs *is addressing the* **Kids.**

Briggs: Now the folk who run these places provide a good and valuable service to travellers like us . . . so remember what I've said.

10   Back at the café

The café is alive with activity: the shutters are coming down, the 'Coaches Welcome' sign is replaced by 'Absolutely no Coaches' and the 'Open' sign by one saying 'Closed'. The doors are locked and bolted; **Mrs Roberts** *and the* **Waitress** *lean against the door.*

11   In the coach

The coach has pulled up. The **Driver** *and* **Mrs Kay** *are looking at the café.*

Mrs Kay: Perhaps it's because it's so early in the season. Maybe if they knew there was the chance of some business they'd open for us. I'll go and give them a knock.

12   In the café

Inside, the two women are silent, terrified. They hear footsteps coming up the drive. The door is knocked upon. **Mrs Kay** *is on the other side of the door watched by the* **Kids** *from the coach windows. She knocks again.*

Mrs Roberts: [*From within*] We are closed!
Mrs Kay: You couldn't possibly. . . .
Mrs Roberts: [*Firm*] We are closed.

[**Mrs Kay** *moves away. As the two women hear the receding footsteps, they sigh*]
Mrs Roberts: I only ever did it once, take a Liverpool coach load. I tell you not one word of a lie Miss Powell, they'd rob your eyes if you wasn't lookin'.

[*The coach pulls away. The* **Kids** *give V-signs to the café and cross their legs to stop themselves from wetting*]

13   A café and shop

*On the window a sign reads: 'Under New Management'. Inside,
two men,* **John** *and* **Mac**, *are behind the counter generally preparing their place for the season.*

John: Look, how many times, listen, it's only the start of the
season innit? Eh? Course it is. We can't make a bloody fortune
before the season's begun, can we?

Mac: See, it's no that what's worryin' me. What I think, see, is
we bought the wrong place. If you was askin' me, I'd say the
coaches'll stop at the first café they come to. An' that's up the
road.

John: Some of them will, yeh. But there'll be enough for us as
well. Give it a month, that's all; y' won't be able t' see this
road for coaches. Thousands of schoolkids with money t'
burn. We'll clean up, mate.

[They hear the sound of brakes and of tyres pulling up. **John**
looks out of the window]

Now what did I say, eh?

Mac: *[Looking out of window. Brightening]* Look at that.
Christ, there's hundreds of them.

John: Right. Let's go. Come on.

[Moves to the counter and points out the items quickly]

John: Jelly Babies: fifteen p. a quarter.

Mac: I thought they was only twelve.

John: Ice creams nine p.

Mac: They was only seven p. yesterday.

John: Listen, mate, can I help inflation?

Mac: *[Getting the picture]* Oh right. I get the picture.

John: Passin' trade mate. Always soak the passin' trade. Y' never see them again so it don't matter. Bubble Gum two p. − no, make that three. Ice lollies ten p. Come on . . . get those doors open. We'll milk this little lot.

14   In the car park

The **Kids** *are tumbling off the coach.* **Mrs Kay** *takes out a flask and sits on a bench in the café garden.* **Briggs** *is frantic.*

Briggs: Stop! Slater, walk . . . walk! You, boy . . . come here. Now stop. All of you . . . stop!

Mrs Kay: [*Pouring out coffee*] Mr Briggs, they'll. . . .

Briggs: [*To a boy,* **Ronson**, *who is rushing for the door of the shop*] Ronson! Come here!

[**Ronson** *stops and walks back to* **Briggs**, *shrugging*]

Mrs Kay: Mr Briggs . . . as long as they don't go near the road I don't think there's any. . . .

Briggs: All right, Mrs Kay.

[**Ronson** *stands in front of him*]

Now just where do you think you are?

[**Ronson** *is puzzled*]

Well?

[**Ronson** *looks round for help in answering. There is none*]

Ronson: [*Sincerely*] Sir, Wales?

15   Inside the shop

The counter cannot be seen for pushing, impatient **Kids**. *The two men are working frantically as orders are fired at them from* *all quarters. As the orders are shouted, the* **Kids** *are robbing stuff left, right and centre − it's the usual trick but the two men are falling for it − the* **Kids** *point to jars high up, as the men turn their backs, so racks of chocolate bars disappear into eager pockets.*

16 Outside the shop

Briggs: And don't let me catch you at it again. Now go on. Walk.

[*He watches as* **Ronson** *walks into the shop. Satisfied, he turns to* **Mrs Kay**]

Now, Mrs Kay, what was it you wanted?

Mrs Kay: Well, I just thought you might like to have a sit down away from them for a few minutes.

Briggs: To be quite honest, Mrs Kay I think we should all be inside, looking after them. Do you think it was wise just letting them all pour in there at once?

Mrs Kay: Ooh ... leave them. They've been cooped up for over an hour. They'll want to stretch their legs and let off a bit of steam.

Briggs: I don't mind them stretching their legs. It's not the children I'm concerned about.

Mrs Kay: Well, just who are you concerned about?

Briggs: There's not only our school to think about, you know. There's others who come after us and they're dependent upon the goodwill of the people who run these places.

Mrs Kay: [*Pouring out another cup of coffee*] Considering the profit they make out of the kids I don't think they've got much to complain about.

Briggs: [*Taking cup*] Thanks. [*Pause*] You know, I'll have to say this to you, Mrs Kay, there are times when I really think you're on their side.

[*Pause*]

Mrs Kay: And I'll have to say this to you, Mr Briggs, I didn't ask you to come on this trip.

Briggs: No, but the Headmaster did.

17   Outside the coach

The last few stragglers climb on board.

Mrs Kay: [*To the* **Kids**] Are you the last? Anyone left in the toilet?

Susan: [*As she finishes counting heads*] That's the lot. We've got them all.

Mrs Kay: All right Ron.

Driver: Right love. [*Starts engine*]

18   In the shop

The **Kids** *have gone and the shelves are almost bare. The two men sit back, exhausted but satisfied.*

Mac: If I hadn't seen it with m' own eyes.

John: I told y'.

Mac: We'll have to re-order.

John: An' that's just one coachload.

Mac: We must've took a bloody fortune.

John: There was sixty quid's worth of stock on those shelves an' most of it's gone.

Mac: Come . . . let's count up.

[*He gets up, goes to the till and opens it. It contains a lot of change but hardly any notes. He is puzzled*]

Was you lookin' after the notes?

John: Which notes? I thought you was takin' care of them.

Mac: Well, we must of taken a load of notes.

[*He looks at the bare shelves*]

19   Inside the coach

The **Kids** *are weighed down with sweets.*

20   The shop

Mac: The thievin' little bastards!

[*He rushes for the door.* **John** *follows. As he flings back the door he sees the coach just pulling away down the road. They run after the disappearing coach. The back window is a mass of two-fingered gestures. The two men are finally left standing in the road*]

21   In the coach

Mrs Kay *leaves her seat and goes over to* **Susan's** *seat.* **Susan** *is playing 'I Spy' with a couple of girls who are sitting with her.*

[**Briggs** *moves across to talk to* **Colin**. *He is conspiratorial*]

Briggs: You know what her problem is, don't you?

Colin: [*Trying to keep out of it. Looking out of window*] Mm?

Briggs: Well, she thinks I can't see through all this woolly-headed liberalism, you know what I mean? I mean, all right, she has her methods, I have mine but I can't see why she has to set herself up as the great champion of the non-academics. Can you? It might look like love and kindness but if you ask me I don't think it does the kids a scrap of good.

Colin: Erm. . . .

Briggs: I mean, I think you have to risk being disliked if you're going to do any good for these type of kids. They've got enough freedom at home, haven't they, with their two quid pocket money and television till all hours, haven't they? [*Pause*] I don't know what you think but I think her philosophy is totally confused. What do you think?

[**Briggs** *waits for an answer*]

Colin: Actually, I don't think it's got anything to do with a philosophy.

Briggs: What? You mean you haven't noticed all this, sort of, anti-establishment, let the kids roam wild, don't check them attitude?

Colin: Of course I've noticed it. But she's like that all the time. This trip isn't organized according to any startling theory.

Briggs: Well what is the method she works to then? I mean, you tell me, you know her better than I do.

Colin: The only principle behind today is that the kids should have a good day out.

Briggs: Well that's all I'm saying, but if they're going to have a good and stimulating day then it's got to be planned and executed better than this.

[*While* **Briggs** *is talking,* **Mrs Kay** *has moved to have a word with the* **Driver**. *Suddenly the coach swings into a driveway.* **Briggs** *is startled and puzzled*]

What's this . . . where are we. . . .

Mrs Kay: It's all right, Mr Briggs ... I've checked it with the Driver. I thought it would be a good idea if we called into the zoo for an hour. We've got plenty of time.

Briggs: But I thought this trip was organized so that the kids could see Conwy Castle.

Mrs Kay: We'll be going to the castle after. [*To the* **Kids**] Now listen, everybody. As a sort of extra bonus, we've decided to call in here and let you have an hour at the zoo.

[*Cheers*]

Briggs: Look, we can't. . . .

Mrs Kay: Now the rest of the staff and myself will be around if you want to know anything about the animals – mind you, there's not much point in asking me, because I don't know one monkey from the next.

Reilly: [*Shouting from back*] Apart from Andrews, miss, he's a gorilla.

[**Andrews** *gives him a V-sign*]

Mrs Kay: And yourself, Brian, the Orang Utang.

[*The* **Kids** *laugh.* **Reilly** *waves his fist*]

Digga: Don't worry, miss, he's a big baboon.

Mrs Kay: Now let's not have any silly name-calling.

Briggs: [*Whispering in* **Mrs Kay**'s *ear*] Mrs Kay. . . .

Mrs Kay: [*Ignoring him*] Now as I was saying, I don't know a great deal about the animals but we're very lucky to have Mr Briggs with us because he's something of an expert in natural history. So, if any of you want to know more about the animals you see, Mr Briggs will tell you all about them. Come on, leave your things on the coach.

Kid: Agh, great.

[*The* **Kids** *begin to get up*]

22   The zoo

The **Kids** *wander around in groups – pulling faces at the animals, pointing and running, girls walking arm in arm. They point and shriek with horrified delight at the sexual organs of monkeys.* **Mr Briggs** *is with a group of* **Kids** *looking at a large bear in a pit.*

Briggs: . . . and so you can see with those claws it could give you a very nasty mark.

Andrews: An' could it kill y', sir?

Briggs: Well, why do you think it's kept in a pit?

Ronson: I think that's cruel. Don't you?

Briggs: No. Not if it's treated well. And don't forget it was born in captivity so it won't know any other sort of life.

Ronson: I'll bet it does, sir.

Girl 1:   How do you know? Sir's just told y' hasn't he? If it was born in a cage an' it's lived all its life in a pit, well, it won't know nothin' else so it won't want nothin' else, will it?

Ronson: Well, why does it kill people then?

Andrews: What's that got to do with it?

Ronson: It kills them cos they're cruel to it. They keep it in a pit so when it gets out it's bound to be mad an' wanna kill people. Don't you see?

Andrews: Sir, he's thick. Tell him to shurrup, sir.

Ronson: I'm not thick. If it lived there all its life it must know, mustn't it, sir?

Briggs: Know what?

Andrews: Sir, he's nuts.

Ronson: It must know about other ways of living, sir. Y' know, free, like the way people have stopped it livin'. It only kills people cos it's trapped an' people are always stood lookin' at it. If it was free it wouldn't bother people at all.

Briggs: Well, I wouldn't be so sure about that, Ronson.

Andrews: Sir's right. Bears kill y' cos it's in them t' kill y'.

Girl 2:   Agh come on, sir . . . let's go to the Children's Zoo.

Andrews: Let's go to the big ones.

Briggs: It's all right . . . we'll get round them all eventually.

Girl 1:   Sir, we goin' the Children's Zoo then.

Briggs: If you want to.

Girl 1:   Come on.

[**Briggs** *starts to walk away. The two girls link his arms, one on either side. He stops*]

Briggs: Oh! [*Taking their arms away*] Walk properly.

Girl 2:   Agh ey, sir, the other teachers let y' link them.

[**Mrs Kay** *is with another group. She sees* **Briggs**]

Mrs Kay: Oh hello. How are you getting on? They plying you with questions?

Briggs: Yes, they've been very good.

Mrs Kay: I'm just going for a cup of coffee. Do you want to join me?

Briggs: Well I was just on my way to the Children's Zoo with these.

Andrews: It's all right, sir. We'll go on our own.

Mrs Kay: Oh come on. They'll be all right.

Briggs: Well, I don't know if these people can be trusted on their own, Mrs Kay.

Mrs Kay: It's all right, Susan and Colin are walking round and the place is walled in. They'll be all right.

Andrews: Go on, sir. You go an' get a cuppa. Y' can trust us.

Briggs: Ah! Can I though? If I go off for a cup of coffee with Mrs Kay can you people be trusted to act responsibly?

[*Chorus of 'Yes, sir'*]

Briggs: All right Mrs Kay. We'll trust them to act responsibly.

Mrs Kay: Come on.

[*They walk off to the zoo café*]

23   The bird house

Two boys are slowly repeating, 'Everton, Everton' to two blue and yellow macaws.

Boy: Go on, just tweek it out, you dislocated sparrow . . . speak!

24   The children's zoo

The **Kids** *watch a collection of small animals – rabbits, gerbils, guinea pigs, bantam hens – all contained in an open pit.* **Ronson** *looks fondly at a rabbit.*

Ronson: They're great, aren't they?

Carol: They're lovely.

Ronson: [*Bending over and stroking a rabbit*] Come on . . . come on. . . .

Carol: Ey' you. Y' not supposed t' touch them.

[**Ronson** *answers by picking up the rabbit and gently stroking it.* **Carol** *reaches over to join him stroking the rabbit but he pulls it close to him protectively*]

Carol: Well. I'll get one of me own.

[*She bends down and picks up a guinea pig which she strokes affectionately*]

These are better anyway!

25   The zoo café

Mr Briggs *and* **Mrs Kay** *are waiting for coffee at the service rail.*

Briggs: How many sugars, Mrs Kay?

Mrs Kay: Call me Helen. I hate being called Mrs Kay all the time. Makes me feel old. I tried to get the kids to call me Helen once. I had the class full of them chanting it. Two minutes later they were calling me Mrs Kay again. No, no sugar, thank you.

26   The children's zoo

More **Kids** *have followed* **Ronson's** *example. Quite a few of them are now clutching furry friends.*

Carol: I'm gonna call mine Freddy. Hiya, Freddy. Hello, Freddy. Freddy.

27   The zoo café

Mrs Kay *and* **Briggs** *are sitting at a table; she lights a cigarette.*

Briggs: They're really interested, you know, really interested in the animals.

Mrs Kay: I thought they'd enjoy it here.

Briggs: Perhaps when we're back in school we could arrange something; maybe I could come along and give them a small talk with some slides that I've got.

Mrs Kay: [*Enthusiastic*] Oh, would you?

Briggs: You should have asked me to do something a long time ago.

Mrs Kay: Well, don't forget you've never offered before.

Briggs: To tell you the truth I didn't think the kids who came to you would be too interested in animals.

28   The children's zoo

The animal pit is empty. The children have gone.

29   The coach

Briggs *and* **Mrs Kay** *approach.*

Briggs: Don't worry, we'll get that arranged as soon as we get back to school.

[**Susan** *and* **Colin** *stand by the coach with the* **Driver**]

Colin: [*To* **Driver**] You should have come round with us, it's a grand zoo.

Driver: ⸱ A couple of hours kip – seen it all before.

Colin: You'd have had a good time.

Mrs Kay: All on board?

Susan: Yes. We wandered back and most of them were already here.

Mrs Kay: Oh! That makes a change.

Briggs: All checked and present. Right. Off we go.

[*The* **Driver** *and the teachers climb on board. In the distance* *the* **Animal Keeper**, *polo-necked and wellied, runs towards the coach. Inside the coach the* **Kids** *sit like angels. The coach pulls away but the* **Animal Keeper** *waves it down. It stops. The* **Keeper** *strides on board*]

Mrs Kay: Have we forgotten something?

Keeper: Are you supposed to be in charge of this lot?

Mrs Kay: Why? What's that matter?

Keeper: Children. They're not bloody children. They're animals. That's not a zoo out there. This is the bloody zoo, in here!

Briggs: Would you mind controlling your language and telling me what's going on.

Keeper: [*Ignoring him and pushing past him to the* **Kids**] Right. Come on. Where are they?

[*The* **Kids** *look back innocently*]

Call yourselves teachers. You can't even control them.

Briggs: Now look. This has just gone far enough. Would you tell me exactly what you want please?

[*A clucking hen is heard. The* **Keeper** *turns and looks. A* **Kid** *is fidgeting with his coat. The* **Keeper** *strides up to him and pulls back his coat, revealing a bantam hen. Two more* **Keepers** *come on board. The first* **Keeper** *grabs the hen and addresses the* **Kids**]

Keeper: Right! And now I want the rest!

[*There is a moment's hesitation before the flood-gates are opened. Animals appear from every conceivable hiding place. The coach becomes a menagerie.* **Mrs Kay** *raises her eyebrows to heaven. The* **Keepers** *collect the animals.* **Briggs** *stares icily*]

30   The coach, moments later

Briggs *is outside talking to the* **Keepers**, *who have collected all the* *animals in small cages. They walk away and* **Briggs** *climbs onto the coach. His face is like thunder. The* **Kids** *try to look anywhere but at him – trying to avoid the unavoidable.* **Briggs** *pauses for a long, staring, angry and contemptuous moment.*

Briggs: I trusted you lot. [*Pause*] I trusted you. And this, is the way you repay me. [*Pause*] I trusted all of you, but it's obvious that trust is something you know nothing about.

Ronson: Sir, we only borrowed them.

Briggs: [*Shouting*] Shut up, lad! [*Pause*] Is it any wonder that people won't do anything for you? The minute we start to treat you as real people, what happens? That man was right, you act like animals, animals! [*Pause*] Well I've learned a lesson today. Oh, yes, I have. I've learned that trust is something you people don't understand. Now, I'm warning you, all of you, don't expect any more trust from me!

[*The* **Kids** *are resigned. They have heard it all before.* **Briggs** *turns to* **Mrs Kay**]

Mrs Kay. When we get to the castle we'll split up into four groups. Each member of staff will be responsible for one group.

[**Mrs Kay** *looks at him*]

31   Conwy Castle

Briggs, *with a group of ordered children standing behind him, points to a spot high up on the castle. The* **Kids** *all look up, bored.*

Briggs: Now you see these larger square holes, just below the battlements there – well, they were used for . . . long planks of wood which supported a sort of platform, and that's where the archers used to stand and fire down on the attackers of the castle. Now what's interesting is, if you look at the side of that tower it's not quite perpendicular. What's perpendicular mean?

Milton: Sir, sir.

Briggs: All right, Milton.

Milton: Straight up, sir. [*Sniggers from the other boys*]

[*In another part of the castle,* **Kids** *are rushing about playing medieval cowboys and Indians.* **Mrs Kay** *sits on a bench overlooking the estuary.* **Carol** *and* **Andrews** *are with her. In a secluded passage of the castle,* **Reilly** *and* **Digga** *are smoking; they are concealed in an alcove.* **Colin's** *voice can be heard. He approaches,* **Karen** *and* **Linda** *follow close behind him*]

Colin: So, although these walls are nearly fifteen feet thick in places, you still have the wind blasting in through the arrow slits and with no proper heat, you can imagine just how cold it must have been.

Linda: Sir, I wonder what they did to keep warm in the olden days?

Colin: [*Stopping and turning*] Well, obviously they. . . . Where's everybody else gone? Where are the others?

Karen: Sir, they kept dropping out as you were talkin'.

Colin: Oh God.

Linda: It's all right, sir. Y' can keep showin' us round. We're dead interested.

Colin: [*Sighing*] All right Linda . . . what was I saying?

Linda: Sir, y' was tellin' us how they kept warm in the olden days.

Colin: [*Continuing down the passage*] They wore much thicker clothing . . . All right, Linda?

Linda: Sir, it's dead spooky. It's haunted isn't it?

Colin: Don't be silly.

Linda: Sir, I'm frightened [*Linking his arm for protection*]

Colin: Now, don't do that, Linda!

Linda: [*Holding on*] But I'm frightened, sir.

Karen: [*Grabbing his other arm*] Sir, so am I.

Colin: [*Firmly, freeing himself*] Now, girls, stop being silly. Stop it. There's nothing to be frightened of! Now, come on.

[*He leads them along the passage. As they pass the alcove where* **Reilly** *and* **Digga** *are concealed,* **Reilly** *leans out and just gently touches* **Linda's** *shoulder. She screams and flings herself at* **Colin, Karen** *reacts and does the same. Even* **Colin** *is slightly startled*]

Linda: Sir, it touched me.

Colin: What did?

Linda: Oh, it did.

[**Colin** *looks worried. They hear laughter. Just at the point when the three of them are about to run,* **Reilly** *and* **Digga** *fall laughing out of the alcove. In the distance* **Briggs** *shouts, 'Reilly!'* **Reilly** *and* **Digga** *hear him and leg away past* **Colin** *and the terrified girls. Outside,* **Mrs Kay, Carol** *and* **Andrews** *still sit looking out over the estuary*]

Mrs Kay: Why don't you go and have a look around the castle grounds. You haven't seen it yet.

Carol: Miss, I don't like it. It's horrible. I just like sittin' here with you, lookin' at the lake.

Mrs Kay: That's not a lake, love. It's the sea.

Carol: That's what I meant, miss.

Andrews: Miss, wouldn't it be great if we had something like this round ours. Then the kids wouldn't get into trouble if they had somewhere like this to play, would they?

Carol: Miss. Couldn't have nothin' like this round our way could they?

Mrs Kay: Why not?

Carol: Cos we'd only wreck it, wouldn't we?

Andrews: No, we wouldn't.

Carol: We would, y' know. That's why we never have nothin' nice round our way – cos we'd just smash it up. The Corpy knows that so why should they waste their money, eh? They'd give us things if we looked after them, but we don't look after them, do we?

Andrews: Miss, miss, y' know what I think about it, eh, miss.

Mrs Kay: Go on, John. What do you think?

Andrews: Miss, if all this belonged to us, miss, and it was ours, not the Corpy's but, ours, well, we wouldn't let no one wreck it would we? We'd defend it.

[**Briggs** *approaches, obviously angry*]

Briggs: You two . . . off! Go on. Move.

Carol: Sir, where?

Briggs: Anywhere, girl. Just move. I want to speak to Mrs Kay. Well, come on then.

[*The two kids,* **Carol** *and* **Andrews***, wander off.* **Briggs** *waits until they are out of hearing range*]

Mrs Kay: I was talking to those children.

Briggs: Yes, and I'm talking to you, Mrs Kay. It's got to stop, this has.

Mrs Kay: What has?

Briggs: What has? Can't y' see what's goin' on? It's a shambles, the whole ill-organised affair. Look at what they did at the zoo. Just look at them here.

[*All around the castle they can see, from where they sit,* **Kids** *running, pulling, laughing and shouting*]

They're just left to race and chase and play havoc. God knows what the castle authorities must think. Look, when you bring children like ours into this sort of environment you can't afford to just let them go free. They're just like town dogs let off the lead in the country. My God, for some of them it's the first time they've been further than Birkenhead.

Mrs Kay: [*Quietly*] I know. And I was just thinking; it's a shame really, isn't it, eh? You know, we bring them to a crumbling pile of bricks and mortar and they think they're in the fields of heaven.

[*Pause. He glares at her*]

Briggs: [*Accusing*] You *are* on their side aren't you?

Mrs Kay: [*Looking at him*] Absolutely, Mr Briggs. Absolutely!

Briggs: Look! All I want to know from you is what you're going to do about this chaos.

Mrs Kay: Well, I'd suggest that if you want the chaos to stop, then you should stop seeing it as chaos. All right, the Headmaster asked you to come along – but can't you relax? There's no point in pretending that a day out to Wales is going to furnish them with the education they should have had long ago. It's too late for them. Most of them were rejects on the day they were born, Mr Briggs. We're not going to solve anything today. Can't we just try and give them a good day out? At least we could try and do that.

Briggs: [*The castle looming behind him*] Well, that's a fine attitude isn't it? That's a fine attitude for a member of the teaching profession to have.

Mrs Kay: [*Beginning to lose her temper ever so slightly*] Well, what's your alternative? Eh? Do you really think there's any point pretending? Even if you cared do you think you could educate these kids, my remedial kids? Because you're a fool if you do. You won't educate them because nobody wants them educating. . . .

Briggs: Listen Mrs Kay. . . .

Mrs Kay: No, you listen, Mr Briggs, you listen and perhaps you'll stop fooling yourself. Teach them? Teach them what? You'll never teach them because nobody knows what to do with them. Ten years ago you could teach them to stand in a line, you could teach them to obey, to expect little more than a lousy factory job. But now they haven't even got that to aim for. Mr Briggs, you won't teach them because you're in a job that's designed and funded to fail! There's nothing for them to do, any of them; most of them were born for factory fodder, but the factories have closed down.

Briggs: And I suppose that's the sort of stuff you've been pumping into their minds, is it?

Mrs Kay: [*Laughing*] And you really think they'd understand?

Briggs: Listen, I'm not going to spend any more time arguing with you. You may have organized this visit, but I'm the one who's been sent by the Headmaster to supervise. Now, either you take control of the children in your charge or I'll be forced to abandon this visit and order everyone home.

[*Pause. She looks at him*]

Mrs Kay: Well . . . that's your decision. But I'm not going to let you prevent the kids from having some fun. If you want to abandon this visit then you'd better start walking because we're not going home. We're going to the beach.

Briggs: The beach!!

Mrs Kay: We can't come all the way to the seaside and not go
down to the beach!

[*She turns and walks away*]

32   The beach

Briggs *sits on a rock apart from the main group.* **Mrs Kay** *is
paddling, dress held above her knees looking old-fashioned, with a
group of kids. Girls are screaming in delight and boys are laughing
and running. Two boys,* **Kevin** *and* **Jimmy**, *are near* **Mrs Kay**.

Jimmy: 'Ey, miss, we could have brought our costumes an' gone
swimmin'.

Kevin: We could go swimmin' anyway, couldn't we, miss?

Carol: [*Trailing behind* **Mrs Kay**]   Miss, when do we have to go
home?

Jimmy: What? In your undies?

Kevin: Yeh. Why not?

Mrs Kay: No. Not today.

Kevin: Agh . . . why not, miss.

Mrs Kay: Because. . . .

Jimmy: If y' went swimmin in just y' undies, the police would
pick y' up, wouldn't they, miss?

Mrs Kay: Look, the reason I don't want you to go swimming is
because there aren't enough staff here to guarantee that it
would be safe. I want to go home with a full coachload thank
you.

Carol: Miss, when d' we have t' go. . . .

Kevin: Agh, miss, I'd be all right, miss . . . I wouldn't get drowned, miss.

Mrs Kay: [*Warning*] Kevin!

Kevin: Oh, miss.

Mrs Kay: Kevin, I've already explained why I don't want you to go swimming. . . .

Kevin: Oh . . . Miss. . . .

Mrs Kay: Carry on like that and I'll have to sort you out.

Kevin: Agh. . . .

[*She stops him with a warning look. He tuts. Satisfied that he won't take it any further, she turns to* **Carol**]

Mrs Kay: Right. . . .

Kevin: Just for five minutes, miss.

Mrs Kay: [*Turning and walking towards him*] Kevin Bryant . . . come here.

Kevin: [*Backing away. Laughing*] Ah, miss, I didn't mean it . . . honest miss. I never meant it.

[**Mrs Kay**, *glaring in mock seriousness, comes after him. He is laughing. He breaks and runs. She chases him, skirts trailing in the water, with the other kids shouting and jeering and urging her to catch him.* **Kevin** *is hardly able to run because of laughing so much.* **Mrs Kay** *charges on through the water, looking incongruous.* **Kevin** *suddenly stops, turns, bends down in the water and prepares to send up a spray*]

Kevin: Don't, miss . . . don't or I'll spray y'.

Mrs Kay: Kevin Bryant . . . you'll do what? . . . You wait till I get hold of you.

[*They face each other. The* **Kids** *at the water's edge chant and shout: 'Get him, Miss', 'Duck him, Miss', 'Throw him in', 'Y've had it now, Bryant'.* **Kevin** *makes the mistake of turning to the group of* **Kids** *to answer them. In a flash she is on him and* *turns him upside down. She ducks him and he comes up sluttering and laughing. The other* **Kids** *cheer and laugh*]

Kevin: Oh no, miss.

Mrs Kay: Now who wanted to go swimming, Kevin?

Kevin: Oh miss, miss. Me 'air's all wet.

[*She quickly lifts him so that she is carrying him, cradle fashion, out of the water.* **Briggs** *looks on. He turns away.* **Mrs Kay** *and* **Kevin** *walk away from the water. He shakes water from his hair*]

Kevin: Miss . . . I might get a cold though. I hate that.

Mrs Kay: Oh, you're like an old woman. Come on then.

[*She reaches in her bag and produces a towel. She wraps the towel round his head and rubs vigorously. Beneath the towel* **Kevin** *is beaming and happy*]

Kevin: Ta miss.

Carol: [*At side of* **Mrs Kay**] Miss, when do we have t' go home?

Mrs Kay: What's the matter, love? Aren't you enjoying it?

Carol: Yeh, but I don't wanna go home. I wanna stay here.

Mrs Kay: Oh, Carol, love . . . we're here for at least another hour. Why don't you start enjoying yourself instead of worrying about going home.

Carol: Cos I don't wanna go home, miss.

Mrs Kay: Carol, love. . . . We have to go home. It can't be like this all the time.

Carol: Why not?

Mrs Kay: [*Looks at her. Sighs*] I don't know, love.

33 The rocks

Colin *and* **Susan, Linda** *and* **Karen** *and some other kids are searching among the rocks.* **Reilly** *and* **Digga** *are nearby with a smaller group of followers. They are having a smoke behind a large rock.*

Andrews: Gis a drag.

Digga: Go an' buy some.

Andrews: Don't be sly, come on.

[**Reilly** *blows smoke in their faces. As they rush for it, he drops it and stubs it out in the sand with his foot. The* **Kids** *fight for it.* **Reilly** *turns away and looks out from the rock. He shouts across to* **Colin** *and* **Susan's** *group*]

Reilly: All right, miss.

[**Colin** *and* **Susan** *look up*]

Colin: [*Quietly*] Ah, here we go.

Reilly: [*Shouting over*] You comin' for a walk with me then, miss?

Colin: [*Standing and pointing. Shouting*] Look . . . I'm warning you, Reilly.

Susan: Don't shout.

Colin: I'm just getting sick of him, that's all.

Susan: Well, why don't you go and have a word with him?

Colin: I don't know. I just can't seem to get through to friend Brian. For some reason he seems to have it in for me.

Susan: I wonder if I could get through to him.

Reilly: Come on . . . what y' scared of?

Susan: You go back with the others.

Colin: What are you goin' to. . . .

Susan: Go on.

[**Colin** *moves off.* **Susan** *walks slowly across to* **Reilly**]

Linda: Has miss gone t' sort him out, sir?

Karen: He needs sortin' out, doesn't he, sir?

Linda: He's all right really, y' know, sir. Y' know, when he's on his own he's great.

Karen: Ooer . . . how d' you know?

Linda: Shut up you.

Colin: All right. All right.

[**Reilly** *smiles.* **Susan** *continues to walk slowly, provocatively, determinedly, towards him. As* **Susan** *stares straight at him,* **Reilly** *smiles bravely.* **Reilly**'s *smile gradually disappears as she gets closer. She steps straight up to him – almost against him.* **Reilly** *looks anywhere but at her*]

Susan: [*Deliberately husky*] Well, Brian . . . I'm here.

Reilly: 'Ey, miss.

Susan: I'm all yours . . . handsome!

Reilly: Don't mess, miss.

Susan: [*Putting her arms around him*] I'm not messing, Big Boy. I'm serious.

[**Briggs,** *in the distance walking along the beach, stops and looks. He sees them then turns and goes back. Meanwhile,* **Reilly** *squirms*]

Susan: What's wrong?

Reilly: I was only havin' a laugh, miss.

[*Lots of little faces peer at them from around and on top of the surrounding rocks*]

Susan: You mean . . . don't tell me you weren't being serious, Brian.

Reilly: I was only jokin' with y', miss.

Susan: [*Keeping him pinned to the rock, quietly in his ear*] Well, you'd better listen to me Brian: [*Pause*] You're a handsome lad, but I'd suggest that in future you stay in your own league instead of trying to take on ladies who could break you into little pieces. All right, we'll leave it at that shall we?

Reilly: Yes, miss.

[*She pats him gently on the face. She pulls back and as she begins to walk away the laughter breaks out.* **Reilly** *lunges out and the* **Kids** *scatter.* **Susan** *turns and sees this*]

Susan: Brian.

[*He looks up and she motions him over. She is now the teacher again*]

You know what we were saying about leagues?

Reilly: Yeh.

Susan: Well have you ever thought whose league Linda's in?

Reilly: [*Smiling*] Linda Croxley?

[**Susan** *nods.* **Reilly** *smiles*]

Agh 'ey miss, she doesn't fancy me. She's nuts about sir. No one else can get a chance.

Susan: I wouldn't be too sure about that.

[*Turns to go*]

See you.

Reilly: See y', miss.

[*He turns and walks back to his mates. As he appears they all start laughing and jeering. He stands smiling and proud*]

Reilly: Well! At least I'm not like you ugly gets. [*A pause during which he grows about two feet*] I . . . am handsome!

34 The beach

A game of football is in progress. **Mrs Kay** *is in goal. She makes a clumsy save and the* **Kids** *cheer.* **Briggs** *watches from a distance.* **Mrs Kay** *leaves the game and goes to meet* **Colin** *and* **Susan** *who are approaching.*

Mrs Kay: Wooh . . . I'm pooped.

Andrews: [*Shouting from game*] Agh, miss, we've not got a goaly now.

Mrs Kay: [*Shouting back*] It's all right, Carol can go in goal for you now.

[*She looks amongst the group.* **Colin** *and* **Susan** *look on*]

Where is she?

Susan: Who?

Mrs Kay: Carol. She went to look for you.

Colin: We haven't seen her.

Mrs Kay: Well, where is she?

[**Mrs Kay** *scans the beach.* **Carol** *cannot be seen.* **Mrs Kay** *looks at* **Susan**]

You haven't seen her at all?

[**Susan** *shakes her head*]

Mrs Kay: [*Looks over beach again*] Oh she couldn't. Could she?

Susan: Lost?

Mrs Kay: Don't say it. Perhaps he's seen her.

[*She shouts across*]

Mr Briggs . . . Mr Briggs.

[**Briggs** *looks up, rises and then comes over to her*]

Susan: I hope he has seen her.

Mrs Kay: Yeh. The only trouble is she didn't go that way.

Briggs: [*Approaching*] Is that it? Are we going home now?

Mrs Kay: Have you seen Carol Chandler in the last half hour?

Briggs: Look! I thought I'd made it quite plain that I was having nothing more to do with your outing.

Mrs Kay: Have you seen Carol Chandler?

Briggs: No. I haven't.

Mrs Kay: I think she might have wandered off somewhere.

Briggs: You mean you've lost her.

Mrs Kay: No. I mean she might have wandered off.

Briggs: Well, what's that if it's not losing her? All I can say is it's a wonder you haven't lost half a dozen of them.

Colin: Listen, Briggs, it's about time someone told you what a burke you are.

Briggs: And you listen, sonny. Don't you try telling me a word because you haven't even earned the right. Don't worry, when we get back to school, your number's up. As well as hers. [*He motions to* **Mrs Kay**] And you, [*To* **Susan**] I saw what was going on between you and Reilly. When we get back, I'll have the lot of you!

Mrs Kay: Would you mind postponing your threats until we've found Carol. At the moment I'd say the most important thing is to find the girl.

Briggs: Don't you mean *try* and find her?

Mrs Kay: Susan ... you keep these lads playing football. We'll split up and look for her.

[**Mrs Kay**, **Colin** *and* **Briggs** *walk off in separate directions*]

35   The cliff

*Below the cliff-top, the sea is breaking on rocks in a cave mouth.
In the distance,* **Mrs Kay** *is shouting 'Carol, Carol', and* **Colin** *is
searching the far end of the beach.* **Carol** *is standing on top of the
cliff watching the waves below. She looks out over the sea. Alone
on the cliff-top, she is at peace with the warm sun and small
breeze upon her – a fleeting moment of tranquillity.*

Briggs: Carol Chandler!

> [**Briggs** *approaches. On seeing her he stops and stands a few
> yards off*]

Just come here.

> [*She turns and stares at him*]

Who gave you permission to come up here?

Carol: No one.

> [*Turning, she dismisses him*]

Briggs: I'm talking to you, Carol Chandler.

> [*She continues to ignore his presence*]

Now just listen here, young lady. . . .

> [*As he goes to move towards her, she turns on him*]

Carol: Don't you come near me!

Briggs: [*Taken aback. Stopping*] Pardon!

Carol: I don't want you to come near me.

Briggs: Well, in that case just get yourself moving and let's get
down to the beach.

> [*Pause*]

Carol: You go. I'm not comin'.

Briggs: You what?

Carol: Tell Mrs Kay that she can go home without me. I'm stoppin' here . . . in Wales.

[*Pause*]

Briggs: Now just you listen to me — I've had just about enough today, just about enough, and I'm not putting up with a pile of silliness from the likes of you. Now come on. . . .

[*He starts to move towards her. She takes a step towards the edge of the cliff*]

Carol: Try an' get me an' I'll jump over.

[**Briggs** *stops, astounded. There is an angry pause. She continues to ignore him*]

Briggs: Now come on! I'll not tell you again.

[*He moves forward. Again, she moves nearer to the edge. He stops and they look at each other*]

I'll give you five seconds. Just five seconds. One . . . two . . . three . . . four . . . I'm warning you, five!

[*She stares at him blankly.* **Briggs** *stares back in impotent rage*]

Carol: I've told y' . . . I'm not comin' down with y'.

[*Pause*]

I'll jump y' know . . . I will.

Briggs: Just what are you trying to do to me?

Carol: I've told you. Leave me alone and I won't jump.

[*Pause*]

I wanna stay here. Where it's nice.

Briggs: Stay here? How could you stay here? What would you do? Where would you live?

Carol: I'd be all right.

Briggs: Now I've told you . . . stop being so silly.

Carol: [*Turning on him*] What do you worry for, eh? Eh? You don't care, do y'? Do y'?

Briggs: What? About you? Listen . . . if I didn't care, why am I here, now, trying to stop you doing something stupid.

Carol: Because if I jumped over, you'll get into trouble when you get back to school. That's why, Briggsy! So stop goin' on. You hate me.

Briggs: Don't be ridiculous – just because I'm a school teacher it doesn't mean to say that. . . .

Carol: Don't lie, you! I know you hate me. I've seen you goin' home in your car, passin' us on the street. And the way y' look at us. You hate all the kids.

[*She turns again to the sea, dismissing him*]

Briggs: What . . . makes you think that? Eh?

Carol: Why can't I just stay out here, eh? Why can't I live in one of them nice white houses an' do the garden an' that?

Briggs: Look . . . Carol . . . you're talking as though you've given up on life already. You sound as though life for you is just ending, instead of beginning. Now why can't, I mean, if it's what you want, what's to stop you working hard at school from now on, getting a good job and then moving out here when you're old enough? Eh?

Carol: [*Turns slowly to look at him. Contempt*] Don't be friggin' stupid.

[*She turns and looks down at the sea below*]

It's been a great day today. I loved it. I don't wanna leave here an' go home.

[*She moves to the edge of the cliff.* **Briggs** *is alarmed but unable to move*]

If I stayed though, it wouldn't be no good. You'd send the coppers to get me.

Briggs: We'd have to. How would you survive out here?

Carol: I know.

[*Pause*]

I'm not goin' back though.

Briggs: Please. . . .

Carol: Sir, sir, y' know if you'd been my old feller, I woulda been all right, wouldn't I?

[**Briggs** *slowly holds out his hand. She moves to the very edge of the cliff.* **Briggs** *is aware of how close she is*]

Briggs: Carol. Carol, please come away from there. [*Stretching out his hand to her*] Please.

[**Carol** *looks at him and a smile breaks across her face*]

Carol: Sir . . . sir you don't half look funny, y' know.

Briggs: [*Smiling back at her*] Why?

Carol: Sir, you should smile more often, y' look great when y' smile.

Briggs: Come on, Carol. [*He gingerly approaches her*]

Carol: What'll happen to me for doin' this, sir?

Briggs: Nothing. I promise you.

Carol: Sir, y' promisin' now, but what about when we get back t' school?

Briggs: [*Almost next to her now*] It won't be even mentioned.

[*She turns and looks down at the drop then back at* **Briggs's** *outstretched arm.* **Carol** *lifts her hand to his. She slips.* **Briggs** *grabs out quickly and manages to pull her to him.* **Briggs** *wraps his arms around her*]

36   The beach

Susan *still waits anxiously on the beach whilst the* **Kids** *play football. Other* **Kids** *watch the game, including* **Linda** *and* **Karen**. **Reilly** *challenges* **Digga** *for the ball and gets it from him.*

Karen: [*Shouting*] Go on, Digga . . . get him, get him.

Linda: Come on, Brian.

[**Reilly** *gets the ball past* **Digga**, *then around two more defenders, and scores.* **Linda** *cheers;* **Reilly** *sees her and winks.* **Mrs Kay** *and* **Colin** *approach.* **Susan** *looks up in inquiry;* **Mrs Kay** *shakes her head.* **Susan** *sighs*]

Mrs Kay: [*As she approaches*] I think we'd better let the police know.

Susan: Shall I keep them playing. . . .

[*Behind* **Mrs Kay**, **Susan** *can see* **Briggs** *and* **Carol** *in the distance*]

Oh, look . . . he's found her.

Mrs Kay: Oh, thank God. [*She turns and starts hurrying towards them*]

Colin: I'll bet he makes a bloody meal of this.

Susan: I don't care as long as she's safe.

Colin: Yeh, well, we'd better round them up. It'll be straight off now.

[**Mrs Kay** *approaches* **Carol** *and* **Briggs**]

Mrs Kay: Is she all right? Carol, the worry you've caused us!

Briggs: It's all right, Mrs Kay. I've dealt with all that.

Mrs Kay: Where were you?

Carol: On the cliff, miss.

Mrs Kay: On the. . . .

Briggs: Mrs Kay, I've found her. Now will you just let me deal with this.

Mrs Kay: [*Shaking her head as they walk up the beach towards the others*] Carol Chandler.

Briggs: Right.

[*The main group are preparing to leave as* **Mrs Kay**, **Carol** *and* **Briggs** *reach them*]

Briggs: Right . . . come on. Everyone on the coach.

[*General 'tuts' and moans of: 'Why can't we stay', etc.*]

Come on . . . all of you, on.

37   The coach

The staff stand by the coach doors as the **Kids** *file by onto the coach.*

Driver: Right. [*To* **Briggs**] Back to the school then?

Briggs: School . . . back to school?

[**Mrs Kay** *looks up*]

It's only early, isn't it?

[*To* **Mrs Kay**] Anyway, you can't come all the way to the seaside and not pay a visit to the fair.

[**Carol** *overhears them as she climbs onto the coach. She rushes inside*]

Carol: [*Loud whisper*] We're goin' the fair, we're goin' the fair. . . .. Sir's takin' us t' the fair.

[*The word is spread like fire inside the coach. Outside,* **Mrs Kay** *is intrigued – half-smiling*]

Briggs: Play your cards right, I might take even you for a ride on the waltzer.

38   A fairground

Rock and roll music. On the waltzer the **Kids,** *including* **Briggs** *and* **Carol** *together in a car, are spinning round.* **Mrs Kay** *takes a photograph of* **Briggs** *and* **Carol** *climbing out of the waltzer car.* **Mrs Kay, Colin** *and* **Susan, Reilly** *and* **Linda, Digga** *and* **Karen, Andrews, Ronson, Carol** *and some of the other kids are all photographed in a group.* **Briggs** *is snapped eating candy-floss, then again on the highest point of the bigwheel with mock fear on his face and* **Carol** *next to him her eyes closed in happy terror. Then he is photographed playing darts, then with a cowboy hat on handing a goldfish in a plastic bag to* **Carol.**

39   Back at the coach

As the **Kids** *pile onto the coach,* **Briggs,** *still wearing his cowboy hat, stands by the coach door.*

Kids: [*As they get onto coach*]
    Sir, thanks, sir.
    Sir, that was Ace.
    We had a great laugh, didn't we, sir?
    Sir, we gonna come here again?

Ronson: Can we come tomorrow, sir?

Briggs: Oh, get on the bus, Ronson.

[*Everyone is singing as the coach moves along. One of the kids is collecting for the* **Driver**; **Reilly** *has his arm around* **Linda**; **Digga** *is with* **Karen**; **Carol**, *with her goldfish, sits next to* **Mrs Kay**; **Ronson** *has a white mouse; the back seat is now occupied by* **Andrews** *and other kids.* **Briggs** *is also on the back seat – cowboy hat on, tie pulled down and singing with them.* **Mrs Kay** *takes a photograph of them*]

Mrs Kay: Say 'Cheese'.

40 Back in the city

The city can be seen out of the coach windows. Inside the coach the kids are tired and worn out now. Some are sleeping, some are singing softly to themselves, some stare blankly out of the window.

Linda: Y' glad y' came?

Reilly: Yeh.

Linda: It was great wasn't it, eh?

Reilly: It'll be the last one I go on.

Linda: Why?

Reilly: Well I'm leaving in the summer aren't I?

Linda: What y' gonna do?

Reilly: [*Looking out of window*] Dunno.

[*Looks out of the window at the City*] It's friggin' horrible when y' come back to it, isn't it?

Linda: What is?

Reilly: That. [*Nods at window*]

Linda: Oh, yeh. [*Resigned*]

[**Briggs**, *with* **Andrews** *asleep next to him, sees the familiar surroundings and the kids hanging about in the streets. He sits up, puts his tie back to normal, goes to straighten his hair and feels the cowboy hat. He takes it off and puts it on* **Andrews**. *He then takes out a comb and combs his hair; puts on his jacket and walks down the aisle to* **Mrs Kay**]

Briggs: Well, nearly home.

Mrs Kay: [*She is taking the completed film from her camera*] I've got some gems of you here. We'll have one of these up in the staff room when they're developed.

Briggs: Eh? One of me?

Mrs Kay: Don't worry . . . I'm not going to let you forget the day you enjoyed yourself.

Briggs: [*Half laughs. Watches her put the film into its box*] Look . . . why don't you give it to me to develop?

Mrs Kay: Would you?

Briggs: Well, it would save you having to pay for it. I could do it in the lab.

Mrs Kay: [*Handing it over*] I don't know, using school facilities for personal use.

[*He smiles at her and takes the film. He puts it in his pocket*]

41   Outside school

It is evening as the coach turns into the street outside the school and pulls up. **Briggs** *gets out, then the* **Kids** *pour out shouting 'Tarars' and running up the street.* **Reilly** *and* **Linda** *get off the coach together.*

Briggs: Right! Come on, everyone out!

Reilly: 'Night, sir. Enjoyed yourself today, didn't y', sir?

Briggs: Pardon?

Reilly: I didn't know you was like that, sir. Y' know, all right for a laugh an' that. See y' tomorrow sir.

Briggs: Eh – Linda.

[*She stops.* **Briggs** *turns*]

We'll, erm, we'll let the uniform go this time.

[*Pause*]

But Linda, don't let me catch you dressing like that in the future, though.

[*She shrugs and walks off with* **Reilly**. *The other kids make their way home.* **Mrs Kay** *gets off the coach*]

Mrs Kay: Nothing left behind. 'Night Ronny.

Susan: Good night.

[*The coach pulls away. The* **Driver** *toots good-bye and they wave*]

Mrs Kay: Ooh! . . . That's that. I don't know about anyone else but I'm off for a drink.

Colin: Oh, I'll second that.

Susan: Good idea.

Mrs Kay: [*To* **Briggs**] You coming with us?

Briggs: [*The school looming behind him*] Well, actually I've. . . .

Susan: Oh, come on. . . .

Briggs: No . . . I'd better not. Thanks anyway. I've, um, lots of marking to do at home. Thanks all the same though.

Mrs Kay: Oh well, if we can't twist your arm.

[*Pause*]

Thanks for today.

[*She turns and goes to her car accompanied by* **Susan** *and*

Colin. *She pulls away and toots good-bye.* **Briggs** *moves to his own car, puts his hand in his pocket and produces car keys and the roll of film. He looks at the film and then up at the school. He pulls open the film and exposes it to the light, crumples it up and puts it into his pocket. He then gets into his car, pulls away and at the junction turns right.* **Carol,** *walking along the street with the goldfish in her grasp, looks up at the disappearing car*]

The Boy with the Transistor Radio

First broadcast on Thames Television's 'The English Programme' on 21 January 1981.

Characters

Terry Davies, aged 16
Mr Davies, his father
Mrs Davies, his mother
Float Jones, a disc jockey
Headmaster
Teacher
Brian }
Kathy } pupils in Terry's class
Other members of Terry's class
Telephone switchboard girl
Con, a worker in a warehouse
Other factory workers

A scene from 'The Boy with the Transistor Radio'.
© *Thames Television*

The Boy with the Transistor Radio

1 Liverpool

We hear Bill Withers singing 'Lovely Day' and we see film of inner Liverpool: nothing sensational, just the inner city as most of it is – depressed, ill-organized, filthy. There is litter and broken glass; old and new housing aimlessly thrown together.

There are long queues at bus stops, buses packed with people going to work. No school kids are about yet.

We see a house, then an interior view of a bedroom.

Terry, *a sixteen-year-old boy, is lying in bed, awake, staring at the ceiling. As the music ends we hear a disc jockey's voice coming from the transistor radio at the side of* **Terry's** *bed. The disc jockey's name is* **Float Jones.**

Float's voice: OK, OK, it's another bright day, and this is Float Jones with you on the late part of the early show wishing you a good, good morning. [*Jingle*] I didn't hear ya. I said, Good morning.

Terry: Mornin', Float.

Float: That's better. Say good morning and hello to another new day. Go on, say it. . . . Say hello.

Terry: Hello.

Float: It's a good day, it's a fine day, it's a smell-of-the-woods-and-pine day. Go on, throw back that window and have a word with this wonderful day.

2   The kitchen

Mr and Mrs Davies *are getting ready to go out to work.*

Mr Davies: Isn't he up yet?

Mrs Davies: He must be awake; he's got his radio on.

Mr Davies: When hasn't he got it on? I woke up in the middle of the night an' I could hear it then.

Mrs Davies: Here's y' sandwiches. Well, he's only a lad.

Mr Davies: Yeh . . . he's only a lad, but he leaves school next week. What's he gonna do then, when he's got a job?

Mrs Davies: *If* he gets a job. . . .

Mr Davies: Ah . . . I've told y'. I'll get him fixed up in our place. I'm havin' a word with Alex today, try an' get him fixed up in the warehouse.

Mrs Davies: I hope y' can. It's so hard for them these days.

Mr Davies: But he'll have to be up an' out. There'll be no lyin' in bed listenin' to the radio when he's got a job. If I get him a job it's up to him to keep it: get in on time everyday, clock in before the time runs out. An' it's not easy, not these days, not with the buses all full an' the queues growin' bigger.

[*We see a view through the window of archetypal suburban England, the England of the advertisers, heavy with blossom and perfectly in order. Then we hear* **Float**]

Float: Float Jones on 209. It's music, music every day. Music to make you feel good, music to make you feel alive. Get into the clouds with this one.

[*He fades in the guitar solo from 'Feel the Benefit, Part 3' by the group 10cc.*]

Mr Davies: [*Downstairs*] Terry. . . . Terry. . . .

3   Terry's bedroom

Terry *is looking out of the window. We are now shown reality, from* **Terry***'s point of view.*

Terry: [*Lowering the volume of the radio*] What?

Mr Davies: Up!

Terry: All right. [*He turns the radio up*]

Mrs Davies: [*Calling*] Terry. . . Terry. . . .

Terry: [*To himself*] Tch. . . . [*Calls*] What?

Mrs Davies: [*Calling from the foot of the stairs*] We're off. See y' tonight. Listen, son . . . make sure y' in early. Y' dad's gonna find out about gettin' y' in at his place . . . in the warehouse. . . . [*Pause*] Did you hear me, Terry?

Terry: Yeh. [*Turns up the radio*]

Mrs Davies: [*Going*] Tarar.

Terry: [*To himself*] Warehouse! I'm not gonna work in a warehouse, am I, Float? I'm gonna do something like you. I'm gonna do somethin' good, somethin' that makes y' feel as good as the music does.

[*He begins to mime playing a guitar to music. He sees his battered acoustic, takes it and pretends to play it. Then he ventures a note. It clashes with the music from the radio. It's obvious that he can't play. He puts it down again and mimes playing to the music from the radio*]

4   The street

Kids are making their way to school and there are long bus queues. **Terry** *is looking through some railings at a factory warehouse. It could be confused with a prison.* **Terry** *pulls himself away and moves on. He takes a lead from his pocket and plugs it into his ear. We hear the radio.*

Float: It's 209 telling you it's good to be alive. Float Jones looking after you, guaranteeing you a good day all the way with 209, the fabulous frequency, the wonderful waveband. . . . Yes!

5   A school hall

The **Headmaster** *is talking to the gathering.*

Headmaster: And we're getting close to that time of the year when some of you will be leaving us to take jobs. The lucky ones. Yes, lucky. Because in this day and age it isn't easy to get a job, as we all know from the newspapers and television, don't we – you!

Boy: [*Startled*] Yes, sir!

Headmaster: Yes. Those of us who have jobs today have to be grateful.

[*He surveys the mass of faces before him. We see it from his point of view and locate* **Terry** *who is staring, apparently attentively, up at him*] Some of us are in for a shock as well. I'll tell you why; you lads who have resented coming to school, you girls who have complained year in year out about disliking school, you'll change your attitude after you've been out in the world for a couple of years because, believe me, it's not all milk and honey out there, you know. It's not all that the pop magazines and television and the advertisers would have you believe. No. And I'll tell you something – when you walk in through the school gates for the first time you're coming in for eleven, maybe twelve years. But most of you, when you walk into your working life, you're going in for forty years. Yes. Forty years. . . . [*He nods*]

[*Now we see the* **Headmaster** *from Terry's point of view and as we hear the guitar solo from 'Feel the Benefit'.* **Terry** *has his earplug in again. At the end of the song, we hear* **Float***'s voice*]

Float: It's summertime. Yes . . . it's summertime on 209 and the livin' sure is easy.

[*We see the platform from* **Terry***'s point of view. In* **Terry***'s imagination, the* **Headmaster** *has been replaced by* **Float**]

Float: You feel a little down, you feel a little blue. . . . Listen to Float, he'll tell you what to do. Listen to the music on 209 make ya better, make ya feel fine. . . . Just do what ya wanna do. . . .

6   A classroom

Kids are waiting for a teacher. **Terry** *is sitting at the back, leaning back on his chair, looking out of the window. The* **Teacher** *enters.*

Teacher: Mornin'.

Girl 1:   Hia, sir.

Boy 1:   All right, sir.

Brian: What happened to your team last night then, sir?

Teacher: What d' y' mean, 'What happened?' What happened was that we had a referee who'd left his contact lenses out. [*Good-natured laughter and derision from the class*] OK, let's have a bit of hush.... Hey!

[*The class quietens*]

Girl 1:   Ah 'ey ... we're not doin' any work, are we, sir?

Boy 1:   There's no point.

Kathy: We're leavin' next week.

Teacher: Have you got a job yet, Kath?

Kathy: Yes, sir. Our Maureen's got me fixed up at her place – y' know, Clifford's Biscuits.

Teacher: Good, good. What will you be doing?

[*During the following dialogue* **Terry** *becomes bored. He takes out his transistor lead and surreptitiously plugs it in*]

Kathy: Sir, at first I'll be sortin' the biscuits, y' know, the ones that get broke. . . .

Girl 1:   They let y' buy them cheap, y' know, the broken ones.

Kathy: I know. But, sir, y' know, later on, when I've got used to the job, I'll have me own machine an' I'll be makin' proper biscuits then.

[*We hear the song, 'Wonderful World;* **Terry** *is looking out of the window. The school dissolves to a shot of a group of bright young people sitting about on the thick grass in the gardens of a public school. We return to the classroom*]

Teacher: . . . That's great, Brian. You start next week?

Brian: Yes, sir.

Teacher: Good. [*Turns to* **Terry**] Terry . . . what about you?

[**Terry** *is unaware that he is being addressed. We hear music again*]

Teacher: Have you got a job, Terry?

[**Terry** *stares at him but makes no effort to answer. The* **Teacher** *is puzzled*]

Teacher: Terry. . . . Terry!

[*The kids in the class turn and look at him and laugh.* **Brian**, *leaning across, unseen by* **Terry**, *pulls the lead from his ear.* **Terry** *is startled, sheepish*]

Teacher: [*To class*] All right, all right. . . . Calm down. . . .

Kathy: He's always listenin' to that radio, sir.

Teacher: Is he? Well, Terry, if I could just interrupt for a minute or two . . . I was askin' if you had a job yet.

[**Terry** *shrugs*]

Kathy: His Dad's gettin' him a job in their place, sir, in the warehouse.

Terry: No, he's not.

Kathy: Yes, he is. Your mam told me mother an' she told me.

Terry: Y' don't wanna listen to me mother. What does she know about it?

Kathy: That's what she said.

Terry: Yeh, but she doesn't realize. Just 'cos she goes out every day doin' a job that she hates she thinks I'm gonna have to do the same. But I'm not gonna work in a warehouse.

Teacher: Well, what are you going to do, Terry?

Terry: Sir, I'll have a proper job, somethin' dead smart that I enjoy doin'. I'm gettin' a job with travel prospects an' a car. An' when I grow up I'll have a wife who's dead smart with proper, nice kids an' a house in the country an', y' know . . . all that!

Boy 1:   The only house you'll see in the country is the looney house.

[*Laughter*]

Terry: You're the one who should be in a looney house. . . .

Teacher: Ah ah ah. . . . Now! Terry . . . listen, how do you plan to achieve all this?

Terry: What d' y' mean, sir? It just comes to y', doesn't it?

Brian: But y' have to work for it, soft lad.

Terry: Well. . . . I'm gonna work. But I'm not takin' the sort of job you've got, Lino. I'm not clockin' in for the rest of me life. . . .

Brian: Shut it, you . . . soft. . . .

Teacher: Terry! Exactly what sort of job do you have in mind for yourself?

Terry: Sir, somethin' in the music business.

Teacher: The music business?

Brian: Goin' on the stage, are y' Terry lad?

Boy 2:   They wouldn't let him on the landing stage.

Brian: Sir, don't believe him, he's lyin'.

Boy 1:   He's a looney, Sir.

Kathy: Sir, he's not got a job in the music business. He's soft.

Teacher: Terry? Well?

Terry: Well, what. . . . I'm not talkin' to them, they're just jealous.

Teacher: Well, Terry. You've got to admit that this future you've got mapped out . . . it does seem a bit impressive. I mean the music business isn't one you just walk into, is it?

Terry: No.

Brian: See. . . . Don't believe him, sir. . . .

Terry: [*Pause*] But I know someone who's gonna get me fixed up.

Kids: Who? Who is it. . . ? What's his name?

Terry: Never you mind.

Kids: [*Derision*] Ah. . . .

Terry: Sir . . . I know someone in the music business. . . . He's a good friend . . . a really good friend.

Brian: What's his name?

Terry: He's great, sir. Sir, I listen to him cos, cos the things he tells me about, y' know, about, like livin', they're the best things I've ever heard. . . .

Teacher: Well, I'm glad you've been listenin' to someone, because in the five years you've been in this school I don't think you've listened to any of the staff, have you?

Terry: No, sir.

Teacher: Well Terry . . . all this good living that you're telling us about . . . you'd stand a much better chance of achievin' it if you had listened to us.

Terry: But, sir, all you and the other teachers, all you ever told us to do was study, an' work hard an' try our best an' take what we get. An' like sometimes I've tried to do that. . .

Kathy: He's never tried to word hard, sir. . . .

Terry: Yes I have . . . I've tried. . . . You don't know about it, but I have. . . . An' it's no good, cos it's too hard. . . . There's too much against y'. Like if I'd started doin' that when I first come to school, when I was a little kid, I'd be OK. But I didn't. An' it's too late now. I'll never get what I want by just studyin' an' workin' hard. It's just dead lucky for me that I've got a friend like Float.

Kids: [*Stunned*] Who?

Terry: Float.

Brian: Float Jones?

Terry: Yeh.

[*The class shout protests, claiming that* **Terry** *doesn't know him*]

Teacher: [*Getting the class quiet*] Look . . . who. . . ?

Kathy: Float Jones. . . . He's a DJ, sir. . . .

Boy 1:   On the radio. . . .

Boy 2:   How could he know Float Jones, sir? He comes from a different world. . . .

Teacher: Do you know him, Terry?

Terry: Sir, he's a good friend.

[*The* **Teacher** *nods, knowing what* **Terry** *means.* **Terry**, *turning, looks out of the window*]

7 The school grounds

We hear the guitar solo from 'Feel the Benefit'. **Terry** *is lying on the grass. The* **Teacher** *appears and looks down at* **Terry.** *He is mouthing something.* **Terry** *removes the earplug.*

Teacher: Can I have a word with you, Terry?

Terry: [*As if to stand*] Yes, sir.

Teacher: No, it's all right . . . stay there. . . . [*Sits alongside* **Terry**]

Terry: [*Looking at him*] What's up, sir?

Teacher: Listen, Terry, don't you think you listen to that thing a bit too much?

Terry: Why, sir?

Teacher: Well, I mean, there are other things in life.

Terry: I know, sir.

Teacher: Well?

Terry:[*Puzzled*] Well what? [*Pause*] Sir, sir, I'd rather listen to me radio. . . .

Teacher: Yes, but . . . but, I mean, you don't want to start believing in it.

Terry: Sir, why not?

Teacher: Well it's not . . . I mean . . . it's not real, is it? It's not life.

Terry: It is to me.

Teacher: [*Looking at him*] Is it?

Terry: Sir, I'd rather listen to a trannie any day than have to think about the depressin' things.

Teacher: Which depressing things?

Terry: You know, sir.

Teacher: I don't. . . . You tell me. . . .

Terry: You know . . . depressin'. Like, y' know . . . livin' round here. It's hardly paradise, is it?

Teacher: [*Pause*] There are worse places.

Terry: I know, but I live *here*.

[*The* **Teacher** *looks at him.* **Terry** *suddenly smiles*]

Terry: Sir, I don't half feel sorry for you.

Teacher: [*Smiling, puzzled*] Why?

Terry: Well, it's like . . . you've been tryin' to teach us lot for the last five years, haven't y' ? An', like most of us, we're gonna walk out them gates as thick as when we come in, aren't we?

Teacher: Come on . . . you've learnt somethin' since you've been here. . . .

Terry: Oh, yeh. But I mean, there's none of us gonna light up the world as far as brains are concerned. But just think, sir, just think that if you'd been a DJ for the last five years – just think how many people would have listened to y' then, an' they would have listened properly. No talkin' at the back or missin' lessons then. Know what I mean, sir?

Teacher: Well . . . erm . . . er, yes . . . I think so. . . .

Terry: Yeh.

Teacher: Terry . . . listen . . . look. . . . Radios, the music you listen to, the disc jockeys and the advertising – that sort of thing . . . you've got to realize that all that sort of thing is a reflection of a world that is not necessarily accurate. Just because you listen to the radio a lot, Terry, it doesn't mean that you'll live your life in paradise. [*Pause*] I mean, these fellows on the radio station who are telling you that everything's fine, everything's easy and uncomplicated – well, you're not . . . you're not meant to believe it.

Terry: [*Emphatic*] You are, y' know, sir.

Teacher: [*Slightly impatient*] Look, lad ... I'm trying to be realistic and make you see sense. I mean ... the special jobs ... the super jobs, there's only a very few of those going. Most of us have to put up with the ordinary day-to-day jobs – doing the best we can. We might want more; but we've got to be prepared for the fact that we mightn't get it. Understand?

[**Terry** *nods and plugs in his ear-piece*]

Teacher: I mean, the DJs might suggest that you're in Seventh Heaven but you're not ... none of us are. Just because there's a picture of life up on a street poster doesn't mean to say that it's yours for the asking. [*The school bell rings*] Well ... come on ... I suppose we'd better get in. .... Come on now. ... [*He sees some boys at the far end of the field. He shouts*] Come on, you lads ... look sharp. ....

[*The* **Teacher** *walks towards the school building. We hear the final bars of 'Wonderful World' as we watch the stragglers make their way into the school building.* **Terry** *lies back on the grass. At the end of the song* **Float**'s *voice is heard*]

Float: Ah yes ... I said to myself ... what a wonderful world. Right now, just stop whatever you're doing, open your eyes and have a look at that great big wonderful world. [*We look, as instructed by* **Float.** *We see nothing sensational, just the facts, the school and the surrounding streets*] It's a beautiful day on 209, the sun's shining and everything's fine; England ... you're beautiful – isn't she beautiful ... ? Yes. Good to have you along. I'm feeling good, you're feeling good, which adds up to the fact that we're all feeling good ... and that's good. ....

[*As we hear the next disc, we see the smile on* **Terry***'s face and then a view of an archetypal English country setting. We should almost feel the Summer County and smell the Hovis baking. Right there in the centre of a field is a cottage. Coming across the field with large dogs romping around him is a figure. We see that it is* **Terry***. He arrives at the cottage door as his wife and super children appear to greet him. He walks into his house and makes his way through to his den which is rigged as a studio. He sits and lifts the waiting mug of creamy coffee. He sips it and smiles at the goodness of it. He clamps on the headphones*]

8   A café

Terry *is at a table with a cup of coffee. Other kids in school gear appear. A woman is collecting used dishes, wiping down tables. A radio plays music, then a jingle, then:*

Float: Float Jones, with you for the next three hours. And the lines are now open on the Float phone-in. Why don't you give me a ring? If you've got any little interesting story about something that's happened to you today – maybe you've won the pools . . . perhaps you've fallen in love . . . yes. . . . Maybe you've just got a funny story to tell, maybe something happened at the shops or at work. If you wanna tell us about it give us a ring on 733 2929. We'll have a chat and play a dedication. OK. 733 2929. . . . [*Music*]

[*During the above scene,* **Brian, Kathy** *and a crowd of kids from* **Terry's** *class have entered.* **Kathy** *goes to the counter to order for them. The others sit*]

Brian: [*Shouting across to* **Terry**] All right, soft lad. . . . How's Float?

[**Terry** *ignores him.* **Brian** *moves across to* **Terry's** *table*] You know what's wrong with you, Terry, lad? Y' just don't wanna work. You're bone idle, y' just wanna laze around all day.

Terry: I don't.

Brian: Well, why don't y' get a job?

Terry: [*Shrugs*] I'm gonna get one.

Brian: Why don't y' try an' get fixed up in Wilson's where I'm goin'?

Terry: Doin' what?

Brian: They've got a vacancy for someone to make up the boxes. It's dead easy. All y' have to do is put a load of cardboard in this machine an' it comes out the other end as boxes. You could get that job.

Terry: [*Pause*] Float's gonna get me a job. . . .

Kathy: [*Putting down a cup for* **Brian**] You don't know Float. . . .

Terry: I do. . . .

Brian: Y' don't!

Terry: If I don't know him . . . how come I'm always talkin' to him, an' he's always talkin' to me?

Brian: [*Looking at him closely*] All right. Prove it.

Terry: What?

Brian: It's the phone-in, isn't it? It's the phone-in now.

Kathy: Yeh, it is, in the afternoon.

Brian: We'll go to the phone box an' you can phone him

9   A phone box

Terry *is pushing a coin into the slot. The others are outside the box listening to* **Terry's** *radio.*

Terry: Erm . . . erm . . . can I speak to Float. . . ?

[*We hear the end of a record*]

Float: OK. We're doing well today. The music's cool, the world is fine and we've got someone on the line. . . . Line three . . . who's that on line three?

Terry: Float. . . . Float . . . erm it's me, Terry!

Terry: Terry? Terry? Now which Terry is that?

Terry: [*Desperate*] Terry! Float. . . . It's Terry Davies. . . .

Float: Ah . . . Terry Davies . . . why didn't you say so? [**Terry** *looks out at others*] OK, Terry, how are you. . . . Now, has something happened to you today?

Terry: Float, my mates at school said I didn't know you an' so I'm phonin' y' so you can tell them you know me.

Float: Terry . . . you listen to 209, yeh?

Terry: All the time.

Float: Terry, are your friends listening?

Terry: Yeh. . . .

Float: OK, Terry's friends . . . this is for you. . . . I, Float Jones, wish you to know that Terry and I are the best of friends. . . . Isn't that right, Terry?

Terry:[*Looking at the others, beaming*] Yes, Float. . . .

Float: Terry . . . anytime. Just get on the line to 209. . . . This is one for you and your friends. . . .

[*A record is played.* **Terry** *replaces phone, leaves the* *box and walks to the group and removes his radio*]

Brian: Agh.... He doesn't really know y'. He was just sayin' that, that's what they always say.

[**Terry** *walks a short distance from them, turns and smiles*]

Terry: Piss off....

[*He runs off, as they leg after him. Music. We see suburban England of the adverts and a house – it is cosy, inviting; a red glow emanates from its windows.* **Terry** *dressed in cap and mackintosh, briefcase under his arm, is running along the street towards this house, through the gate, down the path and into the porch. He rings the chimes, turns and looks out at the raging weather. He smiles in contemplation of the warming soup and the log fire within. The door opens and we see his mum beaming a welcome.* **Terry** *smiles up at her in thanks and admiration*]

10   Terry's real home: the doorstep

Mrs Davies: Terry ... wonderful news ... you've got the warehouse job. [*Pause*] Come on, come, what's up with y'? Get in out the rain will y'?

11   Terry's home: the tea table

Mr Davies: What d' y' mean y' don't think you'll like it? D' y' think I like it, goin' to work? Your mother? D' y' think most people in this world like goin' to work? The country'd be in a fine state if the people who didn't like their jobs stayed at home!

Mrs Davies: 'Ey ... calm down....

Mr Davies: Calm down?

Terry: I just don't wanna work in a warehouse.

Mr Davies: Well, what do y' want, bright spark?

Terry: I want somethin' better!

Mr Davies: Y' want somethin' better, do y'? Y' in the bottom set, in a comprehensive, you've got no exams or nothin' an' you want somethin' better. . . .

Mrs Davies: Ey . . . ey . . . just. . . . Listen, son, we all want somethin' better. But these days we have to take what we can get. Life's not easy, y' know, son.

Terry: [*Pause*] It is. [*Defiant*] It is if y' know Float Jones an' y' listen to him, an' y' hear the music he plays an' the things he says. . . . It is. . . .

Mr Davies: Who?

Terry: Someone.

Mrs Davies: It's a disc jockey on the radio. . . .

Mr Davies: Oh, is it? [*Leaning towards* **Terry**] Well, I'll tell y' what, bright spark . . . why don't y' ask him to get y' a bloody job?

Terry: [*Getting up from the table*] I will . . . I'm going to. . . .

Mr Davies: Don't be so stupid. . . . Just get these soft ideas out y' head. [**Terry** *goes through to the hall. His dad calls after him*] You've got a job, in our place, in the warehouse, an' y' gonna take it.

[**Terry** *opens the door and runs out. We hear the guitar solo 'Feel the Benefit'. We see* **Terry** *running towards a phone box. It is in use. He runs on to another phone box – it is vandalized. Another phone box –* **Terry** *runs towards it. As the music fades, we hear:*]

Float: OK, Float Jones with you here for the last hour of the phone-in and the lines are open. 733 2929. . . .

[**Terry** *pulls open the phone box door. He shows his relief when he finds the phone is in working order. He dials frantically as we hear the jingle*]

Float: And we have a caller here on line five. . . . Who's speaking?

Terry: [*Desperate, short of breath*] Float, Float . . . it's me, Terry. . . . Listen, Float . . . you've gorra get me that job, quick. . . .

Float: Who's. . . .

Terry: . . . All you've been tellin' me about how great everything's gonna be, well it isn't turnin' out that way an' you've gorra help me, Float. I can't do it on me own. . . .

Float: Who is this?

Terry: Float . . . it's me, Terry. . . .

Float: Look, this is a phone-in. . . . Are you sure you've dialled the right number?

Terry: The job . . . the promises. . . .

Float: OK, we've got a record coming up. . . .

Terry: That world . . . the world you've been tellin' me about.

Float: OK, this is . . . [*Quickly he introduces a record*]

Terry: Float . . . Float, y' not listenin' to me. . . .

[*As we hear music come up, a switchboard girl speaks over the phone*]

Girl: I'm sorry, caller, we don't take this sort of call. Thank you.

Terry: [*Shouting into the phone as it goes dead*] Float. . . . Float. . . . FLOAT. [*He is drowned out by the music*]

12   A warehouse

Through this scene, a radio relays the Float Jones programme to the factory floor. **Terry** *walks past pulling a trolley loaded with boxes. He makes his way to the racks. He consults an invoice sheet and begins selecting boxes and placing them on his trolley. Further down the rack an older worker,* **Con**, *is performing the same task.*

Con: All right, son? Gettin' the hang of it now, are y'?

Terry: Yeh.

Con: Doesn't take long to learn this job. Y' soon get to know the ins an' outs. How long y' been here now?

Terry: Three weeks.

Con: Give it another week an' you'll know all there is to know about this job. It's easy, y' see. Eighteen years I've been doin' this.

Terry: [*Looking at him*] Don't y' get bored?

Con: Nah. . . . I never think about it, son. See, the great thing about a job like this, you can let your mind just roam wherever it wants to. You take me; y' think I'm just liftin' boxes down don't y'? But I'm not. Inside, up here, [*Taps his head*] I'm miles away. I'm fishin' for salmon in Scotland or I'm sippin' cocktails somewhere. Know what I mean?

Terry: [*Looking at him*] Yeh. Yeh. I know what y' mean. I used to be soft, like you.

Con: You what? Y' cheeky little git. [*Pause*] Y' all the same, aren't y' . . . youth! Yeh, well you'll learn. Think I'm soft? Well, yeh, you'll change your mind when you've been doin' this as long as I have. You'll see.

[**Con** *goes off with trolley and* **Terry** *follows him.* **Terry** *unloads his trolley on to a packer's bench. As*

we watch him we hear the music on the radio fade and
Float'*s voice come up*]

Float:　Yeh ... that's a good one. And it's a good day
here on 209. The sun is shining, there's music in the
air, the birds are singing and we haven't a care. It's a
beautiful day ... just take a look out of that window.
[*We see that the warehouse windows have been
painted over*] Yes it's a wonderful day here on 209 and
I'm with you till ... well, I'm with you forever. ...

[*During the above we have seen* **Terry** *look at* **Con**,
finish his unpacking and return to the racks again.
Terry *slowly stops working and stands staring at*
Con. **Terry** *looks at* **Con** *again, then at the radio
speaker. He sees a hammer on the bench*]

Float:　Just listen to the sounds and keep cool. It's
music all the way on the fabulous frequency. You feel
a little down, you feel a little blue, well, I tell you, you
know what to do. ... [**Terry** *reaches for the hammer.
We see a close-up of the speaker*] It's fabulous 20 ...
[*The hammer crashes down on the speaker.* **Terry**
stands with the hammer. Stunned workers look at
Terry. *He drops the hammer and walks away,
watched by the others*]

13　A personnel office

Terry *is being paid off. A girl takes back some of his
wages to pay for the speaker.*

14　A second-hand music shop

There is a book of guitar chords in the window. **Terry**
enters the shop.

15   Terry's bedroom

He enters, picks up his guitar and sets the book in front of him. He begins to try to learn a chord, arranging his fingers on the fretboard. He strums his first attempt. It is atonal. His efforts are painful but determined. Eventually he holds one attempt at a chord. The strumming gradually attains a basic rhythm. It becomes heavier and heavier. It is angry. **Terry** *thrashes the guitar. Superimposed is a film of the pop star Sid Vicious singing 'My Way'. It is angry, threatening, compelling.*

Terraces

Characters

Danny Harris
Susan, his wife
Michael, their son
Eddy ⎫
Joey ⎬ neighbours and drinking mates
John ⎭
Billy, a shopkeeper
Joan ⎫ neighbours
Joyce ⎭
Another shopkeeper
First woman
Second woman
Barmaid
Youngster

Terraces

---

1   A local pub

It is Saturday night: noisy, smoky and brash. The women sit drinking at the tables. The men argue loudly at the bar. Everyone is in competition with the juke box.

Eddy: An' the ball ... now listen, listen ... Tommy Wingfield picked it up at the half-way line. He goes thunderin' past the defence ... just like a rocket. [*The women laugh*]

Joey: [*Supporting* **Eddy**] 'Ey, don't laugh ... that's just what he was like, a rocket.

Eddy: A bloody wizard! But what do their defenders do when they see they can't beat him with skill?

John: Swines!

Eddy: They hack him down, don't they! [*There is a respectful pause*] But does Tommy worry about a bit of violence? No, he's up in a flash, the ball still at his feet an' then he lets go ... Wham! D'y' know, his foot moved so fast it was blurred. The ball leaves it like a missile off a launchin' pad. It goes straight past the goaly, into the back of the net, breaks the net, busts right through the back terrace wall, demolishes a bus, puts a hole in the church steeple, kills fourteen pigeons an' guess what?

Joyce: What, Eddy?

Eddy: [*Slamming down his pint*] It was friggin' offside!

2   Danny's house

It is the same night. **Michael**, **Danny's** *son, is doing a crossword in the paper.* **Danny** *is reading a novel.*

Susan: Are we goin', Danny?

Danny: [*Absent*] Mm?

Susan: Are we goin' down there or not?

Michael: Dad . . . what's a [*reading*] 'Historical gang' beginnin' with *M* . . . three letters?

Danny: [*Looking up, puzzled*] A what? Here . . . let's have a look.

Michael: A historical gang.

Danny: [*Getting up and looking at the paper*] Historical! Hysterical . . . you nutter!

Michael: Oh yeh.

Danny: Mob it is . . . mob! Historical!

Susan: Are we goin'?

Danny: D'you fancy it?

Michael: Dad . . . what's a ten letter word that means 'one who always agrees'?

Danny: Who's supposed to be doin' this crossword?

Michael: Me. But you're helpin' me with it.

Danny: What's it begin with?

Michael: I think I've got the first three letters. I think it starts with CON.

Danny: Well can't y' work it out?

Michael: No!

Danny: 'Conformist', isn't it?

Michael: Is it?

Danny: Yes.

Susan: I thought y'd want to go down to the Grapes so you could celebrate gettin' through to the final.

Danny: That's not celebratin'. It's just drinkin' for the sake of it an' going over every last detail a thousand times. You don't need to celebrate a game of football. The enjoyment's in watchin' the game.

Susan: You're a real killjoy, you are. Other fellers would be overjoyed if their team got through to the final.

Danny: I *am* overjoyed. I just can't see much point in goin' over it again an' again. Eddy an' that lot, they're like a television panel. They go on about it so much I think they enjoy talkin' about the game more than they enjoy the game itself.

Susan: So we're not goin' out?

Danny: I didn't say that. Do you want to go out, love?

Susan: Well, it *is* Saturday night.

Danny: Yes, but do you want to go out?

Susan: Yes. Yes!

Danny: Well get your coat on. If you want to go out, we'll go out.

Susan: Well why didn't you say that in the first place? Come on. I bet it's a riot down there tonight!

3   The pub

The pub is heavy with a sense of occasion. The club doesn't reach the final every season.

John: Well, what I think, Eddy, is that this street

should show its support for the team.

Joey: What are you on about? There's not a family in this street that doesn't support the team.

John: Yes, but what I'm talking about is *showing* support. It's all right supporting the team in silence but we must be *seen* to support them.

Eddy: John's right. It's a great achievement and it must be treated as such. To some people it might just be a game of football, a team, but to me it's a game of . . . of . . . life!

John: Hear hear! A game of life . . . I like that, Ed.

Joey: Well look, why don't we put pictures of the team in all the windows?

Eddy: No . . .! That's what y' do at election time. What we're talkin' about is somethin' serious!

Joey: Well, what do we do then?

Eddy: I don't know but it's gotta be something big, y'know, a bit of a splash with *all* the street involved, even the women.

John: Let's all have a think about it.

[*They all go into earnest thought as* **Danny** *and his wife enter. The women call out to* **Susan** *and make way for her to sit with them.* **Danny** *comes across to* **Eddy** *and co.*]

Danny: All right? Celebration pints all round, is it?

Eddy: What a victory though, Danny, eh, eh?

John and **Joey:**   All right, Danny!

Danny: Four pints an' a vodka an' lime, Jose.

Eddy: Danny, listen, we're tryin' to see if we can sort out some way in which the street can show its support for the lads.

John: Come on Danny, surely you can think of some-thin', with an imagination like yours.

John: Got any ideas, Danny?

Danny: [*Handing* **Susan's** *drink across*] Yeh. Go'n watch the team when they're playin' in the final! [*Lifting his pint*] Cheers!

Eddy: [*Lifting his pint*] Hold on, Danny. [*He stops drinking*] Hold on. [*Raps on the bar*] 'Ey. Let's have a bit of order!

[*Supporting shouts of Quiet, Shush*]

I propose a toast. A toast to the glorious lads in yellow who today created . . . history. To the lads!

[*Everyone reverent:* To the lads.]

An' what about a cheer?

[**Eddy** *starts it and everyone joins in. The bubble of conversation blows up again.*]

No, what I'm talkin' about, Danny, is whippin' up some, y'know, some real *interest* like.

Danny: Y' don't need t' do that.

John: Why not? It'd be good, Danny.

Danny: To me it's the game that's important, John. Y' don't want to be gettin' into all these daft things like pictures in windows an' slogans. It's a game, not something else, not something you go out and paint the streets for.

Eddy: [*Grasping him and it*] That's it! That's it! The whole bloody street, every inch of it in the team's colour!

John: Yellow!

Joey: 'Ey, yeh! A yellow street! Brilliant, Danny.

Danny: [*Laughing*] Get lost! I didn't mean . . .

Eddy: We're on. That's it! Right. [**Eddy** *bangs on the bar for order. He gets it*] Is everyone listenin'?

Danny: Eddy . . . listen . . .

Eddy: Right. Now everyone here tonight knows that today our own team, this street's team, got through to the final. [*There's a thundering cheer*] Well look, we've been talking and we think that this street should show its support for the glorious efforts of our noble lads. [*Everyone cheers wildly*]

John: [*Shouting*] Well, what are we goin' to do, Ed?

Eddy: I'll tell you. I'll tell all of you. [*Pause.*] Is everyone agreed? [*Shouts of agreement*] Right. Billy . . . where's Billy? [*A head pops up from the crowd*]

Billy: Here, Eddy.

Eddy: Billy . . . have y' got any yellow paint in the shop?

Billy: I've got gallons of it. It's been there for years.

Eddy: Will y'open the shop tomorrow? So we can buy it?

Billy: Buy it? Y' won't buy it. For somethin' like this y' can have it for free.

[*A spontaneous cheer for* **Billy**. *The pub talk, excited, starts up again*]

Joyce: Don't tell me. Don't tell me that at long last I'm gettin' me house painted! Ohhh, I can't believe it.

Joan: I'll bet we get reporters around. An' the telly.

Joyce: Oh God . . . I'll have to get me hair done!

Joan: Our street could become famous, couldn't it?

Susan: Do you really think the telly people will come?

Joyce: Well they wouldn't miss something like this, would they? I mean, it's important, isn't it?

4 Danny's house

Early next morning. The curtains are drawn. **Susan** *brings in a cup of tea from the kitchen and puts it by* **Danny's** *side.*

Susan: Joyce reckons the telly cameras might turn up when it's done.

Danny: Eh?

Susan: When the street's painted. [*She laughs*] 'Ey . . . they might even interview some of us. Don't y' fancy seein' me on telly, Danny?

Danny: Don't be soft. The street won't get painted. Well our house won't, anyway!

Susan: And why not?

Danny: Come on. It's just stupid.

Susan: Why?

Danny: Come on . . . it is.

Susan: Why aren't we havin' our house painted?

Danny: Because I don't want it painted.

Susan: Well you bloody misery!

Danny: [*Laughing*] Agh . . . come on.

Susan: Everyone else is painting their house! Why aren't we?

Danny: Everyone *won't* be paintin' their houses. If I'd thought they were serious in there I'd have said something. They'll all have forgotten it by now.

[**Susan** *peers through a chink in the curtains, then opens them triumphantly.* **Eddy** *is revealed up a ladder, painting his house*]

Susan: Oh yes. 'They'll all have forgotten it by now.'

Danny: Mmm?

Susan: Look.

Danny: What?

Susan: Come and have a look.

[**Danny** *gets up and sees* **Eddy** *at work*]

Danny: The bloody nutter!

Susan: Why is he?

Danny: He's round the bend. Nobody else will do it. He'll be embarrassed out of his mind. The only yellow house in the street. The Lone Canary.

Susan: How will his be the only one? Everyone's doin' it.

Danny: You mean everyone *said* they'd do it. What they said they'll do and what they *will* do are two different things.

[**Michael** *comes rushing in. Excited, breathless*]

Michael: Dad . . . Dad . . . When are we paintin' our house? Dad, can I help y'? Everyone in the street's doin' it.

Danny: Listen, Michael, Eddy Wills is not everyone.

Michael: I know. But John Cameron's dad's doin' his house down the other end of the street. An' Peter Wilksy's, an' Morgan's, an' they said all the street's gonna be yellow.

Susan: [*Smug*] Satisfied?

[**Danny** *stretches out of the window to see further down the street.* **Susan** *leans out too, and calls to* **Eddy**]

Susan: Let's have a look, Eddy! Ahhh. It's lookin' lovely, Ed! Just what we need in this street, Eddy, a bit more community spirit.

Eddy: [*Shouting over*] Look at them, they're all gettin'

stuck in now. Where's that feller of yours? Come on,
Sue, kick him out of bed an' get him movin'.

Susan: [*Shutting window*] Come on, Danny, let's get
the ladders. Come on, I'll help you.

Michael: An' me, Dad . . . an' me.

Susan: [*Rushing around looking for brushes*] I've told
you. You fellers should have done something like this
years ago. Women wouldn't moan about football if they
were included a bit more often. Come on.

Danny: Do you *want* the house painting yellow?

Susan: Well everyone's doin' it.

Danny: I didn't ask you that. Do you want the house
painting yellow?

Susan: Danny! I want the house painting like the rest
of the street and if the colour they've chosen is yellow
then I'll have my house yellow!

Danny: Would you have it painted yellow if nobody else
was doin' the same?

Michael: Ah come on, Dad!

Susan: [*Becoming exasperated*] Of course I wouldn't. I
don't even like yellow!

Danny: Good. Because I'm not going to paint this house
yellow.

Susan: And why not?

Danny: Because I don't want to!

Michael: Ah 'ey, Dad!

Susan: *You* don't want to? What do you mean, you don't
want to! It's not up to you. The street's decided. . . .

Danny: Yes! An' *I've* decided I don't want my house
painting.

Michael: Ah that's rotten!

Susan: [*Becoming heated*] I thought you supported the team.

Danny: And will painting my house increase my support? When kids go daubing paint over bus shelters, scrawling the team's name on a wall, does that mean greater support? I support my team all right, but that's got nothing to do with painting a house.

[*Pause.* **Susan** *glares at him*]

Michael: All right then. OK. I'll go an' help Wilksy paint his house!

Danny: Michael!

Susan: Go on. You go, Michael love. You go an' help Mr Wilks.

[*He storms out. To* **Danny**]

You make me sick!

Danny: [*Disgustedly*] Agh . . . this is ridiculous!

Susan: [*Tidying up*] Yes . . . I know.

Danny: Why in the name of God does it have to cause this sort of feeling in the house?

Susan: Well it doesn't, does it?

Danny: Meaning what?

Susan: Meaning when you come to your senses, we'll start bein' civil again. Why do you begrudge your own child a bit of pleasure?

Danny: It's got nothing to do with begrudging pleasure and you know it!

Susan: Oh no I don't. It's all very simple, Danny. You stop being high and mighty. Paint the house, and things can get back to normal.

[**Danny** *looks at her, turns, and goes out*]

5 The pub

It is lunchtime. **Eddy**, **John** *and* **Joey** *sit exhausted, beaming, paint-splattered, with pints in hand.*

Eddy: What a response!

John: It was a great idea, Ed.

Eddy: It'll all be done inside the week.

John: Every house . . . yellow!

Joey: Have y' heard when the cameras are comin', Eddy?

Eddy: What cameras?

John: What cameras? The television cameras of course.

Eddy: What? They're gonna put us on telly?

John: Well think about it. There's not many streets as devoted as ours. Oh yes, the cameras will be here, Eddy. I mean, it's a phenomenon, this.

Eddy: 'Ey . . . it bloody is, isn't it? [*Thinks*] I'll have to get me suit pressed!

Joey: Think they'll interview y' then, Eddy?

Eddy: Well it stands to reason, doesn't it? I mean for God's sake – if the cameramen are here they'll want to interview the architect of the idea, won't they?

Joey: I thought it was Danny's idea?

Eddy: Yes, *Danny* thought of it. But without braggin', I did put flesh and bones on it, didn't I?

Joey: That's true, Eddy.

John: Oh it is . . . it is.

Eddy: [*Thinking*] I wonder who'll be doing the interviewing then?

Joey: I hope it's someone from the sports side.

John: We don't want any of them Robin Days around here.

Eddy: I wonder if it'll be Frank. Y' know, Frank Bough.

Joey: He's a good lad, Frank.

John: Our Muriel was sayin' she hopes it's Russell Harty who comes to interview.

Eddy: Yeh, well that's women for y', isn't it? No . . . it'll be a sportin' man they send.

[**Danny** *enters, crosses to the bar, and orders a pint. He can hear the comments of the others*]

Eddy: I see some people still observe the Sabbath round here.

Joey: Just got up have y', Danny?

[**Danny** *collects his pint and goes across to join them*]

Danny: All right.

John: I hope you've noticed the work that's been done while you've been sleepin'.

Eddy: Better get y' finger out, Danny. Frank Bough's comin' y' know, Dan.

Joey: An' Robin Day.

Eddy: Keep this quiet, Danny, but, er, I've heard they might be devotin' a whole programme to it.

Danny: Listen, Eddy, I think y'd better know. I've got no intention of paintin' my house.

Eddy: [*Pause, puzzled*] What d'y mean?

Danny: What I say. I'm not painting my house.

[*There is a silence in which they all look at him*]

Look, lads. It's quite simple – I *don't want* to paint my house! Now can we just leave it there? [*Pause*] Come on, let's talk about somethin' else.

Eddy: [*Stunned*] Somethin' else!

Joey: What's wrong with y', Danny?

Danny: Nothing's wrong with me, Joe. But I don't want to paint my house.

John: And why not?

Danny: No reason, John. I just don't want to.

Eddy: But Danny, Danny, is it a question of what *you* want?

Danny: It is my house. It's my decision.

John: But you live in a community, Danny. You've got to think of others as well.

Danny: I've thought of others, John, an' if my house remains unpainted it won't hurt one insect, animal or human being.

Eddy: How do you know you won't be hurtin' anyone?

Joey: Frank Bough won't like it.

Eddy: Now come on, Danny lad. Let's stop arsin' round!

[*He puts his hand in his pocket and produces a fiver*]

Here, Joey. Go an' get a few whiskies in.

Danny: Listen, Eddy . . .

Eddy: [*Laughing*] You're a case, you are, Danny. Always were a bit of the awkward one. A bit different. 'Ey, John, I'll bet he was an awkward bugger when he was a kid, eh?

[**John** *and* **Eddy** *laugh*]

Danny: Eddy, y' can laugh, buy whisky for me, bring in a troupe of dancin' girls if you like, but I won't be paintin' my house.

Eddy: [*The laughter fading*] People won't like it, y' know, Danny.

[**Danny** *shrugs*]

John: Why try to be the odd one out, Danny?

Danny: I'm not trying to be anythin', John. [*He sighs*] I just don't want . . . to . . . paint . . . my house.

[**Joey** *arrives with the whisky and places a glass down in front of each man*]

All right? So can we just forget it now? Eh?

[**Danny** *leans forward to pick up his drink. A hand covers the top of the glass before* **Danny's** *can reach it*]

Eddy: No way, Danny!

Danny: What's up?

Eddy: If a feller doesn't want to join in with me, all right. That's OK. But if he's not with me in all things, he's not with me at all.

Danny: For Christ's sake, hasn't this gone far enough? Stop bein' stupid!

Eddy: It's not me that's bein' stupid, Danny. [*Pause*] Now, are y' gonna drink with me?

Danny: [*Pause. He looks at the glass*] I'll drink with you, Eddy.

Eddy: [*Beginning to remove his hand*] Good lad, good lad.

Danny: But I won't paint my house!

Eddy: [*His hand shooting back to the glass*] Well y' won't drink with me either!

[*They look at each other.* **Danny** *suddenly gets up*]

Danny: Y'can stick your friggin' drink!

[**Danny** *heads for the pub door*]

Eddy: [*Shouting after him*] It's up to you, lad. This drink'll still be here at closing time. It's up to you!

6 Danny's house

Danny *is late home. He has been wandering the streets, sorting out his thoughts. Now it is past closing time, and he knows that the drink* **Eddy** *placed on the table as a symbol of togetherness is no longer there to be consumed.*

Danny: Any tea made, love? [*Silence*] Susan . . . any tea? [*Pause*] We're not still carryin' this stupid thing on, are we?

Susan: If you want tea you know where the pot is.

[*She studies the TV screen with unusual intensity.* **Danny** *looks at her, then goes to the kitchen. There's a knock on the door, and* **Eddy** *puts his head round tentatively.* **Joey**, **John** *and several others are behind him*]

Eddy: All right, Sue love, can we have a word with Danny?

Susan: Come on in, Ed. He's in the kitchen.

[*The men stream in. Not a mob: more a deputation*]

Susan: Danny! Eddy's here!

[*Pause. There is no response*]

Eddy: Listen, Danny . . . we've been talkin'.

Danny: [*From the kitchen, making tea*] Have you?

John: We've been a bit rash, Danny.

[**Danny** *comes to the door*]

Danny: Well I'm glad you've realized it, John.

Eddy: Look, Dan. I mean, OK. You don't wanna be bothered paintin' the house. So what we've done, Danny, is a few of the lads an' meself have agreed that we'll do it for y'.

Susan: [*From the back of the group*] Ah . . . now that's what I call real friendship, Eddy.

Eddy: [*Making to go. Others follow*] So we'll get the paint and get stuck in tomorrow, Danny. OK? An' we'll forget about today. All right?

Danny: [*Following them to the door*] Eddy.

Eddy: What's that, Dan?

Danny: You lay one hand, one finger on an inch of my brickwork an' I'll have the coppers round here before you can move!

Susan: Danny!

Eddy: Danny lad! We're offerin' to do you a favour.

Joey: We'll even paint it back to the normal colour when the final's over.

Danny: No thanks.

[*Pause*]

Eddy: I wouldn't push it *too* far, Danny.

Danny: I'm not pushing it at all.

John: Listen, mate. We came round here to make things OK between us. Now if you're gonna start bein' unreasonable. . . .

Danny: [*Closing door after them*] Ta-rar, lads.

Eddy: [*Wedging his foot in door*] I'm warnin' you. You'd better bloody grow up. Or you'll be sorry.

[**Danny** *closes the door*]

Susan: You're warped! Did you know that? Warped, that's what you are. They're your friends.

Danny: No! Friends will let you be yourself!

[*He walks past her and back into the kitchen*]

7 A corner shop

It is next day. **Joyce** *and other women are waiting to be served.* **Susan** *enters.*

Joyce: We're just sayin', Sue. The telly people are coming, you know.

First woman: When's that feller of yours goin' to get started?

Shopkeeper: Russell Harty's comin', isn't he?

Joyce: An' Hughie Greene. Oh' they're all comin'.

Susan: He'll do it. Don't worry.

Second: I heard someone sayin' that Harold Wilson's openin' a school near here on Friday.

Joyce: Go 'way. An' they're bringin' him to see the street?

Second woman: Well they didn't exactly say. . . .

Joyce: I know . . . but he will come, won't he? I mean he always goes to see the interesting things. [*Pause*] Harold Wilson comin' to our street! You'll have to get your feller movin', Sue.

8 A street

Danny *is walking along on the way back from work. Even more houses are painted now. The street is taking on an overall yellow look.*

He walks past **Joey's** *door.* **Joey** *is just putting his key in.*

Joey: [*Whispering nervously*] Danny. 'Ey, Danny.

Danny: [*Stopping*] What?

Joey: [*Checking to make sure he's not being watched*] Come here. I don't wanna be seen. Listen, I don't think they're gonna be comin' till tomorrow, the telly people.

Danny: Yeh. Well?

Joey: Listen, Danny. I'm trying to help you. I shouldn't even be seen talkin' to you, mate. What I'm sayin', Danny, is . . . you've still got time. Y' could get it painted by tonight.

[**Danny** *turns and walks away*]

9   Danny's house

In the living room stand three gallon tins of yellow paint and a large brush. **Danny** *can't miss them.* **Susan** *is sitting in the armchair.*

Danny: What's that?

Susan: Paint.

Danny: I can see that. What's it for?

Susan: You're going to paint this house, Danny.

Danny: Oh am I?

Susan: I'm not going to be humiliated any longer. It's all right for you. You don't get it. You're out at work all day. But I have to live here, in this street. All day, people goin' on at me, makin' me feel small. Well I'm not puttin' up with it any more. Danny, I'm not bein' humiliated again.

Danny: You don't have to be humiliated. Stand by me

and there'll be no humiliation.

Susan: [*Bouncing out of the chair*] I'm not arguin' with y', Danny. I've had enough of bein' the reject. Now listen, I'm giving you a warnin', Danny: either you paint this house tonight . . . or I'm gettin' out!

Danny: Don't be so stupid!

Susan: Stupid! You call me stupid?

Danny: Yes. You're acting like a child.

[*The front door is heard opening.* **Michael**, *tear-stained and screaming, rushes in.* **Danny** *tries to take him, but he runs to his mother*]

Susan: Michael . . . Michael . . . what's wrong?

Michael: [*Between sobs*] They won't . . . they won't . . . play with me . . . they all said . . . an' everyone in school . . . they all said [*Breaking down*]

Susan: Said what, love? What did they say?

Michael: Said our house . . . is a . . . a house for freaks! [*Breaks down*]

Susan: [*Screaming at* **Danny**] See! See what you and your stupid bloody ways have done! [*She puts her arms around the child and leads him to the door*] Don't cry, love. Don't cry. You're right. It is a freak's house. Look, there's the freak . . . y' father! He's the one who's turned it into a house for rejects. Well he'd better do somethin' about it quick or else he'll be the only one livin' here!

[*They exit, leaving* **Danny** *alone in the room.* **Danny** *looks at the paint, sighs, and takes off his coat. He goes into the hall, and returns wearing overalls, and carrying a paint brush in one hand and step ladders in the other.*

He is about to add a gallon of paint to his load when there is a loud bang on the door. A note comes through] *the letter box.* **Danny** *bends down and picks it up]*

Danny: [*Reading*] 'This is a warning! Paint – or find somewhere else to live!'

[**Danny** *screws the note up. He opens the front door and steps out into the street. He places three cans of paint on to the pavement. He stands looking at the houses opposite. All yellow. There is a deliberate 'Western' atmosphere building up]*

Danny: [*Shouting at houses*] Are you all watching? All listening? Are y'? [*Laughs*] Come on . . . come out and have a look. [*Pause*] Where are y'? Come on . . . come on out! [*Pause*] See . . . look . . . the paint's here. Come on, you can come out.

[*Slowly front doors begin to open*]

Come on . . . *all* of y' . . . COME ON!

[*Neighbours begin to emerge*]

See . . . look . . . there's the paint. It's yellow, see. Right? [*Pause*] Now someone wants me to paint my house, eh?

Eddy: [*Shouting across*] I'm glad you've seen some sense, Danny.

Danny: Sense? Oh yes, I've seen sense. [*He stands and surveys the onlookers*] I've seen sense all right. You all want me to paint the house, do y'?

Eddy: Good lad, Danny.

John: Good man . . . good man.

Danny: Watch . . . just watch. [*He slowly bends and prises open one of the cans. He lifts it*]

Eddy: [*To a neighbour*] I knew he'd see sense in the end. [*He turns back to look at* **Danny**. **Danny** *is pouring the paint down the grid*]

Danny: Well that's my answer. That's what I say to you. And just in case you didn't hear me – [*He quickly prises open another can and hurls the paint across the road*] Can you hear my answer now? Can y' [*He shouts loud and clear*] All I wanted to do was leave my house. That's all. [*He grabs the third and final can. Behind* **Danny, Susan** *and* **Michael** *emerge from the house. It is obvious that they are leaving*] Go on . . . Yes . . . you go. Go and join your friends. [*He watches as they cross the street and are comforted and taken in by* **Joyce**]

Eddy: [*Shouting across*] I always thought there was somethin' about you, mate, an' now I know what it is: they build places for people like you – asylums!

[**Danny** *rushes forward and grabs the paint brush. He swings and scoops up paint with it, hurling it all along the street. It is a gesture of total and frustrated anger. There are screams as people try to get out of the way of the flying paint.*

   Danny, *his anger momentarily spent, stands glaring and breathing very hard*]

10   The pub

Eddy, *his cronies and others are drinking at the bar.*

Barmaid: Well I know one thing, he'll never get served in this pub again.

John: [*Shaking his head*] I just couldn't get over it. I thought he was just being a bit stubborn. But did y' see him with that paint? Did y' see him though?

Eddy: He's dangerous if y' ask me.

Barmaid: Who would have thought. I mean, livin' in this street so long and no one would have guessed we had someone like that in the midst of us.

Eddy: He bloody well worms his way into our friend-ship. Drinks with us, laughs with us, goes out with us . . . an' all the time he's pretendin' he's normal.

John: He's not normal. He's a sick man. Sick in the mind.

Joey: Yeh, an', for God's sake, there's half the cameras of the world gonna be beamin' in on us tomorrow.

Barmaid: Not now. No. They won't come here.

Eddy: Why won't they?

Barmaid: They'll go to Wingfield Street. They've copied us, haven't they?

Eddy: Y' what?

Barmaid: All the Wingfield Street end are makin' arrangements to do their street up in the team's colours.

Eddy: But the cameras won't cover them. We were the originals.

John: The originals, yes. But Wingfield Street is gonna be *completely* yellow, Eddy. Not just almost yellow, yellow with a dark blob in the middle.

Barmaid: That's why they'll get all the attention in Wingfield Street.

Eddy: Oh no they won't!

Joey: They will, Eddy. If there's a part of our street not painted they'll go and . . .

Eddy: Yes. But there's not gonna be a part of our street that isn't painted! [*Rallying*] We're not gonna let one feller, one diminished feller, put the boot in on us are we? Eh? Someone should've told Danny Harris that this country is ruled by majorities. We've got no time for the oddballs and queerheads here. I'm bloody sick of the awkward ones, I am – the left-handers and backward walkers. I'm up to here with the awkwardites an' them who think they can do what they like while the rest of us just have to stand by. It's the likes of Danny Harris who've given this country a bad name, who've pulled it down into the muck an' slime. Most of us just get on with things in a quiet an' orderly fashion while the screwballs like him fling spanners in the works. [*Pause*] Well if he doesn't wanna fit in it's his hard luck. We'll have to *make* him fit in.

Joey: What'll we do, Eddy?

Eddy: Right. Listen. Tomorrow ... while he's at work ...

11 Outside Danny's house

Joey *is breezing along, whistling self-consciously, and glancing behind him as he goes. He carries a paint tin and brush. At* **Danny's** *house he opens a can of paint, and starts painting, checking that no one is watching. Satisfied, he relaxes.*

As he does, an upstairs window opens quietly. A bucket appears.

Joey, *still relaxed, whistles while he paints. Suddenly water cascades over him. He looks up and sees* **Danny** *in the bedroom window.*

Joey: Bastard. You bastard, Harris!

Danny: [*Calm*] Come back and you'll get it again.

Joey: [*Pointing up*] We'll get you, Danny Harris ... Don't worry ... We'll get y'. [*He slopes off, angry and dripping wet*]

12   Inside Danny's house

A **Youngster** *knocks at the door.* **Danny** *opens it.*

Youngster: You Mister Harris?

Danny: Yeh.

Youngster: There's a phone call for y' in the pub.

Danny: Who's it from?

Youngster: I dunno. The woman in the pub just sent me down here to tell y'.

Danny: [*Suspicious*] She didn't say who it was from?

Youngster: I think it was from y' wife.

Danny: Me wife?

Youngster: I think that's what she said.

Danny: [*Checking that no one is around*] Right. [*He comes out and closes the door*]

13   The pub

Danny *enters and walks up to the bar.*

Danny: Someone said there's a call for me.

Barmaid: Oh yes . . . there was, Danny . . . they rang off though. Said they'd call back in a few minutes. [*Pause*]

Danny: Was it from Sue?

Barmaid: I don't know, erm, Danny. I didn't answer it, Phil did. Look, why don't you have a drink while you're . . . What'll it be? [*She hands a pint across, and* **Danny** *makes to pay. The* **Barmaid** *pushes the money back to him*]

Barmaid: No . . . go on, Danny . . . have this one on me.

Danny: [*About to drink. He becomes suspicious and*

lowers his drink] How long have you been givin' away
free drinks?

Barmaid: [*Nervy*] Oh . . . y' know.

[*Pause*]

Danny: Who, erm . . . who was it on the phone then . . .?

[**Danny** *idly goes to the window and looks out*]

Barmaid: Erm . . . I don't . . . er . . . I think it was Sue,
Danny.

Danny: [*Quietly walking back from window*] You think
it was Sue? You lying bitch! [*He slams the pint down on
the counter and runs out*]

14   Outside Danny's house

Eddy *and* **Joey** *are painting frantically, up a ladder.*
   Danny *runs up the street.*
   Eddy *and* **Joey** *look down in horror as they see the
paint suddenly being kicked over. They shin down the
ladder and run off.*
   Danny *stands, breathing heavily; glaring, wild.*

15   Inside Danny's house

It is night. **Danny** *is asleep. He turns over, half wakes,
and then, fully-waking, listens to soft sounds creeping in
from outside.*
   *He gets up, goes to window and sees a large group of
men below, preparing to paint.* **Danny** *slips into the
bathroom, clips a hose pipe to the tap. He turns it on,
running the water into a bucket so that he can carry the
hose back to the bedroom window. He quietly raises the
sash, lifts the hose, and a jet of water gushes out into the*

night. The nocturnal decorators scatter, shouting, shocked.

Danny *leaves the hose pipe propped so that it runs out of the window. Then he brings a chair and sits waiting.*

When foxes prowl the farmer must sit the long night out.

16   The pub

Eddy, **John** *and others are standing by the bar, drinking in ominous silence; drinking with a purpose.*

Eddy *lays down his pint and looks at the clock: It is 6.10.*

Joey *rushes through the door.*

Eddy: Right lads . . . let's go!

Joey: Eddy . . . Eddy . . . Eddy . . . I've just heard Royalty's visitin' the neighbourhood tomorrow, Eddy . . . what are we gonna do?

Eddy: Let's go.

Joey: [*Following*] Where, Eddy?

Eddy: [*Leading the group of men*] Just follow me.

17   Danny's house

Susan *is knocking at the front door.* **Danny** *opens it with extreme suspicion.*

Susan: [*Nervous, reluctant almost*] Hya . . . Danny.

Danny: Hello!

Susan: Can I come in?

Danny: Who've y' got with you?

Susan: For God's sake, Danny!

[**Danny** *peeps out, checking that all is clear*]

Danny: All right. Come in.

[*She enters.* **Danny** *closes the door and stands in the hall. There is an awkward silence between them*]

Susan: Well, aren't you going to offer me a cup of tea?

[*He looks at her. Blank*]

Shall I make it? [*She goes through to the kitchen.* **Danny** *follows her*]

Danny: What's all this in aid of then? Have they sent you to try an' change my mind?

Susan: [*Getting tea things ready*] Don't you think you could have thought of Michael and me in all this, Danny?

[*Pause*]

Danny: Couldn't you have thought of me? [*Pause*] We're a family. [*Pause*] We didn't have to do what a street chose to do.

Susan: Where's the cups? I'll bet you haven't washed a dish, have y'? All the cups in the front room . . . Go an' get a couple and I'll wash them.

[**Danny** *goes through to the front room*]

Danny: [*From front room*] Well . . . what have you come here for? Are y' coming back for good?

Susan: [*Quietly unlocking and unbolting the back door*] I'll come back, Danny, when you see sense and paint the house. [*Pause*] You're just like a little boy over all this.

Danny: [*Appearing at kitchen door with two mugs*] I've missed you. And Michael.

Susan: Danny! Go on . . . before it's too late . . . just say you'll paint the house. And then we'll come back.

Danny: But can't you see? If I do that there's no point is there? There's no point in you coming back, in us being together.

Susan: Please, Danny . . . please! Before it's too late . . . please!

Danny: What do y' mean, 'before it's too late'?

[*And in answer the back door opens.* **Eddy** *and a group of men burst in.*

   Danny *looks at* **Susan. Susan** *looks away*]

What have y' done? What have you done?

Susan: I'll come back, Danny . . . when it's painted. We'll be all right then, Danny.[*She goes out of the back door*]

[*The men grab* **Danny**, *and there is a struggle as he is forced into the street outside.*

   Someone has picked up a straight-backed kitchen chair, and **Danny**, *forced to sit in it, is tied to it with rope.*

   Eddy *and the men begin to paint the house rapidly*]

Eddy: We're sorry it had to come to this, Danny. It hurts us more than it does you. But we hope it makes y' see sense, Danny. I want y' t' know, Danny, that when this is over, we can all go back to bein' mates. You had to be knocked back in line, Danny. But when this is over there'll be a drink waitin' for y' in the pub.

[*In no time at all* **Danny's** *house is yellow, like every house in the street.*

   Danny *sits in the chair, slaughtered.*

   Eventually he struggles up as the men pick up their tools and leave for the pub. The ropes fall loosely to the ground]

Eddy: [*Calling from the other end of the street*] Don't forget your pint, Danny lad!

[**Danny** *looks at the house. He turns away in the opposite direction*]

I Read the News Today

First broadcast on BBC School Radio in the series 'Listening and Writing' on 4 February 1977

Characters

Ross, a local radio disc jockey
Voice (of a radio commercial)
Ronny, a youth on the run
Police constable
Police sergeant
Newscaster
Interviewer

Willy Russell is indebted to the Beatles for the title of this play, taken from their song of the same title.

I Read the News Today

---

1 A local radio station

Ross, *a disc jockey, is at the microphone.*

Ross: OK. That's er . . . my Record of the Week. Don't think it'll be too long before that one's riding high in the national charts.

[*Music*]

And this is Paul Ross, with you until the crack of dawn. And tonight, I've got a deserted studio. Night Spin, tonight – it's just between ourselves . . . Let's cut out for a short break, before I bring you the news.

Voice [on tape]: An orchestra? A band? A group? No. Just one man and one instrument can produce the sounds you hear. The SOUNDPACK! A revolution in music. With absolutely no knowledge of music, YOU can produce sounds like this:

[*Muzak*]

And this:

[*Muzak*]

SOUNDPACK is not just an instrument. It's a band at your fingertips. Have you ever wanted to produce great music, but not known how? Then SOUNDPACK is for you. SOUNDPACK – no knowledge of music required. SOUNDPACK – available at music shops, and most large department stores.

[*Muzak fades*]

Ross: OK, Paul Ross back with you here on Night Spin. And it's time for the halfway news. [*Takes on a more formal news reader voice*] A dramatic escape in the city today. After being sentenced to eighteen months detention, a local youth made a dramatic escape from police who were leading him from the city's magistrates' court. The youth, Ronald Arthur Heron, made his successful bid for freedom by jumping from a moving police van after magistrates had convicted him of causing more than five thousand pounds' worth of damage to goods in a local warehouse. In an act of what the magistrates called 'mammoth, unprovoked, mindless vandalism', Heron had single-handedly smashed an entire floor of goods belonging to Pine Cash and Carry Ltd. A police spokesman said that he expected Heron to be apprehended 'before very long'. Local ratepayers met council officials tonight in an effort to reduce rates in the city. A spokesman . . . a spoke . . .

[*The sound of a slight scuffle*]

Ronny: Don't move! Right, just don't move, or y' dead. Right?

Ross: Am I movin', man? Eh? Look, I mean . . . I'm not moving. Don't shoot me. Please, whatever you want, you can have it. Don't shoot me . . . please.

Ronny: I won't shoot, if you don't move. I don't wanna hurt you, so just be a good lad, an' do as y' told. . . . Right . . . slowly . . . move that chair back . . . Listen, mate . . . tell me the truth. Is there any rope, tape, anythin' like that in here?

Ross: [*Terrified*] I don't know . . . man, I . . . I don't know . . .

Ronny: What's up with you? Are y' gonna cry? I'm not gonna hurt you. Are you worried about the gun? Well, just be a good lad, an' I won't have to fire it. Come on, is there any rope in here?

Ross: What for?

Ronny: What for? What d'you think for? So we can play skippin' games! I wanna tie you up, that's what for.

Ross: There's . . . there's cable . . . you could use that.

Ronny: Good thinkin', Batman.

Ross: Look . . . there's some spare cable down there . . .

Ronny: Get up slowly, an' pass it to me.

Ross: I hope you . . . I hope you realize that when you cut the transmission you probably alerted half the city that something was wrong down here.

Ronny: That's all right. Sit down there. As soon as I've got your feet tied to this post, you'll be goin' back on an' tellin' them it was just a technical hitch. Right? You just tell them it was a fault, an' then stick an LP on. All right, put y' feet together. Right, now tie them to that post.

Ross: You've not gone to all this trouble just to get something played on the radio have you?

Ronny: Don't try an' be smart, you.

Ross: I'm sorry, man . . . Look, I just . . .

Ronny: All right. Yeah. Maybe I am doin' all this just t' get somethin' played on the radio. Not a record, though. I couldn't care less about records. Just put anythin' on. But listen, mate. Do anythin' wrong an' you get this . . . straight through the head. Right?

Ross: Look, man . . .I've told you . . . I'll do just what you say, and nothing more . . . honestly.

Ronny: Right. I'll tell you what to say.

2   A police station

Constable: 'Ey, Sarge.

Sergeant: What?

Constable: I've just had about half a dozen calls sayin' the local radio station went off the air without any warnin'.

Sergeant: Well, why are they ringin' us? Tell them to ring the radio station. Not the police station. We're coppers here. Not electricians. I don't know . . .

Constable: They say they can't get through. The telephone line's dead, as well.

Sergeant: Wouldn't you think we had enough to cope with, eh? Get the transistor out the back. Let's have a listen.

3   The radio studio

Ronny: An' when you've told them that, I want you to put the record on. Then switch it so that it's only the record that's goin' out of here. I don't want them to hear us. Right?

Ross: I'll do whatever you say . . .

Ronny: Good. 'Cos I don't wanna have to shoot you. OK. Go on.

Ross: Paul Ross . . . er . . . here again with . . .er . . . apologies for the loss in transmission. We've got the engineers in here trying to sort out what went wrong, and . . . er . . . well, here's a record while they try and sort out the problem.

4   The police station

Sergeant: What did I tell you? Put it off. I hate that rubbish.

Constable: Sorry, sarge, but we had to . . .

5   The radio studio

Ronny: All right. OK, pal. Now just take it easy.

6   The police station

Sergeant: 'Ey! Hold on. Just switch that up.

7   The radio studio

Ronny: [*Pointing to the panel of controls*] 'Ey! What's that switch? It's still up.

Ross: Which switch?

Ronny: Which switch? That switch.

Ross: Look, man. You want the record transmitting. We can't transmit anything without that.

Ronny: Those microphones aren't on, are they?

Ross: Of course not. Look, I'll speak into them. If they were live, you'd hear it amplified in the studio . . .

Ronny: You just leave them alone. I'll try them, not you. Hello . . . hello . . . testin', one, two, three, testin' . . .

Ross: I've told you man, they're dead. The only thing going out is the record.

Ronny: Yeah . . . What's in that, that cubicle thing over there?

Ross: That's the teleprinter. The news comes in on that.

Ronny: I'm gonna have a look. Don't try anythin'.

8 The police station

Constable: Shall I get a car round, Sarge?

Sergeant: Eh? What for?

Constable: Well you just heard it.

Sergeant: What you talking about? It's just a play isn't it? That's all. Switch it off.

9 The radio studio

Ross: [*speaking into the microphone*] A gun . . . he's got a . . . gun . . . he's got a . . .

[*The sound of paper rustling*]

Ronny: 'Ey . . . they're still lookin' for me.

Ross: What?

Ronny: Look, it's just come through on that typin' machine. 'Local police are still on the lookout for the youth who escaped outside the city's magistrates' court today. The youth, Ronald Arthur Heron, had been convicted of causing more than five thousand pounds' worth of damage to goods belonging to Pine Cash and Carry Ltd.'

Ross: What! You mean, you mean that's you?

Ronny: Course it is. An' this: listen. 'Reports just coming in that the same warehouse was vandalised tonight. As yet, no confirmation of a link between the two items.'

Ross: What? You escaped, then went back and did it again?

Ronny: Yeah.

Ross: Listen, man. Why hang around here, then? Why don't you split, now?

Ronny: They'd only catch me, wouldn't they?

Ross: But look, man, can't you see that you'll be caught if you hang around here?

Ronny: You think I'm thick, don't you? Course I can see that. I'll get caught. I know that. But not till I've told them.

Ross: Told who?

Ronny: Them . . . the people out there. The listeners. See, they never let anyone talk, y'know. Know that magistrate, that judge who did me today, eh? I tried to tell him, I did, you know. But he wouldn't listen. They never do, you know. I tried. I tried to tell him so's it'd get in the papers, an' that. No chance, though. He just started shoutin' an' abusin' me, didn't he. You know the form. 'Mindless'. 'Vandal'. 'Unprovoked'. 'Senseless'. You know, all that stuff. An' I was tryin' to tell him, for cryin' out loud. There was no way he was gonna listen. No way. That's why I did a bunk. It's all lies, you know.

Ross: What is?

Ronny: All of it. It's all lies that they tell you. Like you. You're a liar!

Ross: Listen, man . . .

Ronny: You are, you know. Like all the stuff you put out over the radio. It's all lies, isn't it? All lies an' cheatin' an' that. Rubbish it is.

Ross: Look, I just play the records, and . . .

Ronny: I know what you do. I've listened to you. You even played a dedication for me once. *San Quentin* by Johnny Cash. D'you remember?

Ross: Well . . . er . . . we get lots of requests for dedications . . .

Ronny: For me mam an' our Billy it was. Don't you remember?

Ross: Yeah, yeah, I think I do . . . yeah . . . it's coming back, now.

Ronny: Liar! You never remember anythin' like that. You don't give a thought for anyone who writes in to you. You just read out their dedications, an' then forget about them. You didn't even play *San Quentin*. You played *Boy named Sue* instead.

Ross: Look . . . I'm sorry, man.

Ronny: It's all right. I hate Johnny Cash now, anyway. He's another liar. I used to think he was great. But he was all lies, as well. I found that out, you know. He was supposed to have been in prison an' on drugs an' all that. Supposed to be a hard man. He wasn't, though. He didn't do any of that. He was just a singer. Lived all his life in a hotel in New York.

Ross: Is that right?

Ronny: Yeah. I've had enough of heroes now. Does the gun frighten you?

Ross: I would appreciate it if you could point it elsewhere.

Ronny: I'm not gonna shoot you.

Ross: Look, I know you don't want to shoot me but accidents can happen, can't they?

Ronny: I got it from the warehouse. You know, the

place I did. I found it in a drawer.

Ross: Why did you vandalize the . . .?

Ronny: I didn't vandalize it.

Ross: I'm sorry . . . I meant . . .

Ronny: I know what you mean. I wrecked it, like. I wrecked it, 'cos it deserved wreckin'. It was all rubbish, all of it, but it wasn't vandalism. It was justice. You started it, y'know?

Ross: Look, man, I don't know what you're talking . . .

Ronny: If I hadn't listened to your show, I wouldn't have heard the advert, would I?

Ross: Which?

Ronny: You know which advert. That *Soundpack.* Music at your fingertips. Be a real musician? It's just a box of tapes, isn't it? Pre-recorded tapes, that's all . . . isn't it? Eh? Eh?

Ross: I don't know, man . . .

Ronny: Don't 'man' me! A four-year-old kid could play one of them. You put it out, don't you, as though all you have to do is buy one of them, an' you'll be a great musician. Lies, you see . . . lies again. You press the keys, an' all it does is set off a load of tapes inside. It's not me who's playin' though, is it? Eh? It's the feller who put the music on the tape in the first place, isn't it? He's doin' the playin' . . . not me.

Ross: I'm not responsible for the jingles. You can't blame me for the jingles, man.

Ronny: When I smashed up all them *Soundpack* things in that warehouse, I was doin' people a favour – it wasn't vandalism. But they never listen. Even when you try an' tell people to stop listenin' to the lies, they still go on doin' it. When you tell them that it's a con, all of it, they don't listen to you. They'll listen tonight, though. They'll have to, 'cos I'll be shoutin' it out through every radio in town.

10   The police station

Sergeant: [*On the telephone*] Yes . . . yeah . . . yes . . . I've heard it, madam. Yes. Well I . . . yes . . . yes, I . . . er . . . yes. Well, I think you'll find that it's just a play. A drama. Yes . . . that's right. No need to worry now. OK. Thank you. [*He puts the telephone down.*] I don't know. They can't tell fact from fiction out there.

[*The sound of the telephone ringing*]

Not another. Here, you take this one.

Constable: [*On the telephone*] Yes . . . hello . . . Well, I think . . . Oh. Yeah . . . I see . . . could you just hold on a second, please? [*He turns to the sergeant*] Sarge, I've got a feller here who says that the lad in the studio is the one who jumped the van today.

Sergeant: Rubbish. He's gettin' the news mixed up with the fiction.

Constable: What shall I say?

Sergeant: Here . . . give me the phone. [*He takes the phone*] Hello, sir. Sergeant Morison here . . . yes . . . Well don't worry, sir . . . I'm sure you'll find that it's just an invented thing . . . yes . . . yes, all right . . . OK. Thank you. [*He speaks to the constable*] Switch it on. I don't know. If they're gonna do realistic plays, you'd think they'd give some sort of an explanation first.

Ronny: An' how do I work it so that I'm broadcastin'?

Ross: I'll switch on for you.

Ronny: Right. Go on . . . What's that light goin' on for?

Ross: That's a cue light. It means get ready. When the other light comes on, it means you're live.

Ronny: Go on. Switch on. [**Ross** *switches on*] OK. Is that it? Are we on? All right. OK. Right. This is, er, Ronny Heron here. I've . . . er . . . I've come to tell you about the lies. You know, the lies that you hear all day on this radio station. See, I found out. Like before, when they was puttin' out the news an' they said that I vandalised that warehouse. Well, that was a lie. You'd think the news would be honest, wouldn't you? But it's not. They said that I vandalized that warehouse. But I didn't. I wrecked it. Oh yeah, smashed everythin' up, but it wasn't vandalism. If you bought one of them *Soundpacks* y'd know what I mean.

Constable: I'll get the car, Sarge.

Sergeant: Just hold on.

Ronny: But not only that. Everythin' else is the same. Like, like, you know that advert, the one for the tee shirts, the one where they say all you have to do is get one of these tee shirts, an' then you'll get loads of dates. Well you won't, you know. Wearin' one of them tee shirts won't make any difference at all. People should start to realize that. It's the same with all the stuff they tell you about on this station an' on the telly an' the sides of buses. You know, the stuff that they say'll change your life. Well, listen, it won't. All the tee shirts, an' cars, an' washing machines, an' fridges, an' radios, an' stereos, knife sharpeners, holidays, books, an' make-up, an' things that they sell you – none of it'll ever change you, y'know, if you're no good in the first place. If you're no good, you stay no good. An' the lies that they tell you, the lies about all them things, if you believe them, they just make it worse for you. An' you know what the biggest lie is, eh? You know the biggest lie of all? The music! That's the killer. 'Cos you listen to it, don't you? At night, out there, you listen to the music driftin' out an' it makes you feel good, doesn't it? As though everything's good around you an' inside you. When the music plays, it's as though the world was made for *you*, an', an' tomorrow's gonna be a good day, an' everythin's gonna be all right, an' every road goes somewhere. There's birds singin', an' the moon's always big an' yellow. There's always a girl to love you an' hold you an' look after you forever. It's like that, isn't it, when the music's playin'? But it's only music, you know. It's only a load of tapes in a box, really.

Constable: Shall I get the car?

Ronny: [*On their radio*] I just wanted to tell you that.

Constable: Shall I, Sarge?

Sergeant: I dunno, lad.

Constable: Well, you heard him. It's Heron all right.

Ronny: [*On their radio, to* **Ross**] Switch that off. Switch it off.

Sergeant: How do we know it is Heron? Say it's just a play?

Constable: Well, a play wouldn't be about today's news would it?

Sergeant: That's the sort of thing they do these days. Documentary sort of things. I mean, what I'm worried about is supposin' it is just a play. Suppose it is, an' we get a car round there. I can just see tomorrow's news bulletin: 'Police move in to arrest radio play!' We'd be laughin' stock.

Constable: Sarge, that's not a play. It's happenin' now. It's the truth.

Sergeant: All right, get a car. We'll take a look.

11   The radio studio

Ronny: You know the worst thing, eh, Ross? Eh? I'll tell you. When they pick me up for this one, they'll send me for reports. You know, psychiatrists like. Soft, isn't it? They'll treat me as though I'm mad, because I wanted to tell the truth.

Ross: Look, if you split now you could still . . .

Ronny: No point. I might as well wait here, an' get a free ride to the cop shop.

Ross: You're just gonna give yourself up, quietly? No shooting? Look, man, it'll do you no good. You start letting that thing off, man, an' it's gonna be a lot more than Borstal for you.

Ronny: Start shootin'! I'd have a job, wouldn't I? It's a toy gun! A replica! Some people, I dunno, they'd believe anythin'.

Ross: You could have told me that before, couldn't you?

Ronny: It makes a change though, doesn't it Ross? You bein' fooled for once, instead of you foolin' everyone else. That's prime, that is.

Ross: Listen, you . . . when the coppers get here, you better tell them straight off that that gun isn't real.

Ronny: Why? What you worried about, Ross?

Ross: They might be armed.

Ronny: The coppers! Armed? They're comin' to get *me*. Not Al Capone. You've been watchin' too many films, mate.

Ross: Look. You just tell them as soon as they get here. Right?

Ronny: Since when have you been givin' orders round here?

Ross: Listen, idiot. When you thought we weren't on the air, we were. Right? The police, out there, they'll think you've got a real gun. Why do you think it's taken so long for them to get here? They'll have been organizing armed men to come and get you.

Ronny: You said it wouldn't be goin' out. You said that was the truth. You just can't stop lyin', can you? Why couldn't you just tell the truth for once?

Ross: It's your own fault. You lied to me. You told me that gun was real.

Ronny: I didn't lie. It is real.

Ross: Oh, come on. You . . .

Ronny: I lied when I told you it was a dummy.

Ross: I don't believe you.

Ronny: Don't you? Right! [*He presses the gun to* **Ross's** *head*]

Ross: Take that away from my head.

Ronny: Shall I pull the trigger?

Ross: Look, get that away from my head. Listen, please, please, man . . .

Ronny: I thought you didn't believe me.

Ross: I believe you. Please take the gun away.

Ronny: You better had believe me, an' all. 'Cos the gun is real. An' it's loaded. An' I'm not goin' quietly. I'm goin' out of here shootin'.

Ross: Please let me get out first.

Ronny: Why? You're my passport, Ross. My passport to freedom. With you as a hostage, I can get away from here. I can make them get me a plane.

Ross: You're not gonna try that one. Man, you've been listening to too much news.

Ronny: I'm not goin' to Borstal. If they don't get me a plane out of the country, you're a dead man.

Ross: Don't be stupid. That only happens in stories. It's not real.

Ronny: We'll see about that.

Sergeant: Heron!

Ronny: Who's that?

Sergeant: Heron! This is the police. Look through the glass. I'm in the next studio. Can you see me?

Ronny: Yeah. I can see you.

Ross: He can't hear you. Press that switch. Talk through that mike.

Sergeant: Can you hear me, Heron?

Ronny: Yeah. I can hear you . . .

Ross: Don't shoot . . . just don't . . .

Ronny: Shut it, you . . .

Sergeant: Right, lad. Put the gun down.

Ronny: Get lost.

Sergeant: Just put it down, an' no one will get hurt.

Ronny: I decide who gets hurt. Listen. Do what I tell you, an' everyone'll be happy. I wanna get out of here, right? Now I wanna car to get me an' Ross to the airport, an' I wanna plane waitin' to take . . .

Sergeant: Come on, Ronny, lad, you've been listenin' to too many plays. Just come back down to earth, an' everything'll be all right.

Ronny: Oh, it'll be great, won't it! Everything'll be wonderful! I'm tellin' you, either I get out of here to a waitin' plane, or I do Ross in.

Ross: Please . . . please do as he says . . .

Ronny: That's right . . . do as I say, or Ross gets it.

Sergeant: I don't believe that you'd do that, Ronny.

Ronny: Well you better had believe me.

Sergeant: Come on, Ronny. I'm coming in there now . . .

Ross: Don't . . . please . . .

Ronny: I'll shoot him . . . I'm tellin' you . . . Don't you try it. Get back! I'm warnin' you . . . get back . . .

Sergeant: [*Coming into the studio*] Right, Ronny, give me the gun.

Ronny: Get out! Get back! I'll put one in you first . . .

Sergeant: No you won't! Come on . . . come on . . . now . . .

[*The sound of a scuffle*]

Right . . . hold him, constable. Good lad, hold him there. You all right, sir?

[**Ross** *sighs with relief*]

Sergeant: Who were you gonna shoot with this, Ronny? Mm? You would have been better off with a water pistol. Didn't anyone tell you, Heron, if you're gonna shoot anyone, you have to get a real gun first. Come on, let's be havin' you.

12   The radio studio

It is the next day.

Newscaster: This is Peter French with the mid-day news. Following last night's dramatic scenes here at Radio Ford, a youth, Ronald Arthur Heron, has appeared before a special magistrates' court. Heron, who said nothing during the two minute hearing, was remanded for psychiatric reports. For the full details of last night's drama we go over to the man who was at the centre of the ordeal, Radio Ford's DJ Paul Ross.

Ross: Perhaps the most terrifying experience I've ever gone through. The . . . er . . . the worst thing about it was when, as lots of listeners will have heard, he started ranting on about truth, you know. Er . . . I mean, I knew then that I was dealing with someone who was totally unpredictable.

Interviewer: You mean, you got the impression that he was disturbed?

Ross: Yeah. I . . . well . . . you know, I knew then that I was dealing with a madman.

[*The sound of John Lennon and the Beatles singing* I Read the News Today *fades in and drowns out* **Ross** *and the interviewer*]

Follow-up Activities

The discussion topics suggested for each play may of course be considered in either large or small group discussion. When the latter is the case, those taking part may each note their own answers, opinions and conclusions; or the group may try to reach a consensus and one 'reporter' could note the group's answers.

Our Day Out

Discussion

1   Do the kids dislike Briggs? Are they afraid of him? Do they resent his strictness? Do all of them?
2   Do you think he is too strict? If so, when? Is he ever justified?
3   Why does he behave as he does at the fairground?
4   How do you think he will behave the next day at school?
5   Why does Mrs Kay behave as she does?
6   Do you think she is ever too easy-going? If so, when? Is she 'good' for the kids? Would some people think her 'irresponsible'? Do you?
7   Do you think she is right just to want to give them a good day out?
8   What do you think of the various kids? Are they

justified in their behaviour? (For example, in the shop and at the zoo?)

9　Why does Reilly behave as he does towards Susan?

10　Why do you think Carol behaves as she does at the cliff?

11　Do the kids deserve freedom and trust? If you were one of their teachers, how would you treat them?

12　How do the teachers in the play compare with ones you have known in the past?

13　In which parts (if anywhere) do you think this is an exaggerated picture of such a day out?

14　Do you think the day out was a good idea? Is it a 'success'? (Has it done any lasting good? Did Mrs Kay expect it would?)

15　One teachers' magazine has attacked the play for including the 'racist' remarks made by Digga and Reilly on page 28. Willy Russell says he does not hold those characters up for approval but wants to show that they have adopted racist attitudes from people around them. In that way, they are 'typical'. The lines are certainly (and sadly) all too realistic. Do you think plays should show life 'as it is'?

Improvisation

1　Scenes which might take place at school the next day – especially conversations between:
(a) Briggs and the Headmaster;
(b) Mrs Kay and the Headmaster;
(c) Mrs Kay and Briggs;
(d) Briggs and Carol;
(e) Briggs and a group of the older kids;
(f) the kids who went on the outing and those who didn't.

2　The staffroom meeting that might be held to discuss the outing.

3   Scenes from a school outing you have been on.
4   The whole class could combine to make its own play
    about a school outing. Before beginning, plan care-
    fully the roles each person will play and decide on the
    'places' to be visited. Besides including scenes at
    these places, include the conversations that would
    take place before the outing, while travelling and
    (perhaps) on returning.

Writing
1   Write the conversation that Linda and Reilly have as
    they walk home together.
2   Write (in playscript form) the scene in the pub as Mrs
    Kay, Susan and Colin talk over the day. Think
    carefully about what will seem most important to
    each of them and what any of them might want to
    ask each other.
3   Suppose that, after the coach has left the zoo, the
    keepers tell their local paper about what happened.
    The reporter cannot interview anyone from the
    school because the keepers did not know the name of
    the school nor did they notice the name of the coach
    company (although they would have recognized the
    Liverpool accents). But the reporter can interview
    the keepers and get their side of the story. Write the
    report that might appear in that local paper.
4   Suppose the head asks Briggs for a written report of
    the day out. What would Briggs put in the report and
    what would he leave out? Write his account of the
    day out.
5   Write the story of a school trip, outing or journey you
    have been on. Just as Willy Russell lets us see the
    day out in his play from both the teachers' and
    pupils' viewpoints, try to let your reader know what

your outing was like for your teacher(s) as well as for you.

The Boy with the Transistor Radio

Discussion

1   Why do you think Terry spends so much time listening to his radio?
2   How does he regard (a) his parents; (b) his school-friends and (c) his teachers?
3   Float talks in a different way to the other characters. Note down some of his 'typical' remarks. What do they show about the way he seems to see the world? What sort of 'personality' is he?
4   Why does Terry change his mind about working in the factory?
5   There are several 'fantasy' sequences in the play. What do they tell us about Terry? What other points do they make?
6   Do you know anyone who believes in a television serial? Or anyone who regards a disc jockey or television personality as a friend? Are such beliefs harmful in any way?
7   Is it good to dream of 'escaping' or is it dangerous to live in a dream world?
8   What does the final scene tell us about what is likely to happen in the future?

Improvisation

What do you think you will be doing in ten or twenty years' time? Imagine your life turns out just as you hope it will. Then improvise (in groups of three) a meeting with two old schoolfriends whom you have not seen since leaving school. You chat about what has happened to each of you since leaving school. Then imagine things have not gone so well. Improvise meeting in those circumstances. Discuss what you could do to help the first scenario come true.

This exercise could be tackled in another way. Imagine first that things do not go well for the first ten years. You meet and chat . . . Then you get your life organized and begin to do well. In another ten years the three of you meet up again. . . .

What would the reverse be like? Ten years' success followed by ten years that are much less successful?

Writing
1 Terry leaves school during the course of the play. Write his end-of-year report (in the style of your school reports).
2 Script a scene in which Terry brings this report home to his parents. (Decide first between which scenes in the play it might occur.)
3 Suppose Terry was able to express his frustration as a poem or in song lyrics. Write his poem or lyrics for him.
4 Some people spend a lot of their time daydreaming. Write a story about someone who 'escapes' into their daydreams: *The Secret Life of.* . . . Perhaps their daydreams are triggered by events around them: a period they are learning about in history, a film on television, an advert on a street hoarding. . . .

Terraces

Discussion
1 Has Danny any obligation to paint his house yellow just because he lives in the same street as the others? Or because he has been friends with them? Is he a 'killjoy'?

2   Should he change his mind once Susan and Michael are made really unhappy?

3   What sort of person is Susan?

4   Why do you think many people want to be 'on the telly'?

5   What is significant about the crossword clues Michael is filling in at the beginning of the play?

6   Are Eddy and his friends a 'mob'? Are they justified in their later tactics?

7   After the end of the play, will they 'all go back to bein' mates'?

8   Why do you think crowds turn out to cheer winning teams? Do you want to join in victory celebrations of teams you have not played for? How – and in what circumstances?

9   What would you have done in Danny's position?

10 Do you admire individuals who take a stand against a crowd or mob or gang? Can you think of examples? When is it dangerous to do so?

Projects

1   Plan, improvise (and record, if possible) the interviews that the television crew might film or tape supposing they did in fact come to the street. Who would they interview? Television reporters are sometimes said to have five favourite questions which begin 'Who . . .?' 'What . . .?' 'When . . .?' 'Where . . .?' and 'Why . . .?' What could be the reporter's complete questions on this occasion? What other, perhaps more interesting questions could be asked?

2   How old do you think Michael is? Suppose he kept a diary. Write *The Secret Diary of Michael Harris, aged* . . . for the period covered by the play.

3   Script the scene between Susan and Danny when they first meet after the final scene in *Terraces*.

4 Suppose Danny never goes into the pub again. Improvise and then script a scene which takes place in the pub two or three months after the events in the play. Eddie and his friends talk over what happened and what has happened since. . . .

5 Write a story about a local event you have seen or taken part in, when 'everyone' seemed to join in. It might perhaps have been a street or school party, a fête or village fair, or a celebration to mark a religious festival or Royal occasion. (Did in fact everyone take part with equal enthusiasm?)

I Read the News Today

Discussion

1 Why did Ronny damage the goods in the warehouse the first time?

2 And why does he do it a second time?

3 Is he justified?

4 Why does he hate the music Ross plays?

5 In what ways is Ross like Float Jones (in *The Boy with the Transistor Radio*)?

6 Do you think Ross is insincere in his regular programmes? Or is he just doing what is expected of any disc jockey? *Can* a disc jockey be sincere?

7 What do you think makes a good disc jockey?

8 Are Ross's listeners 'manipulated' by the music he plays? Do you tend to like music you hear a lot?

9 Who do you think chooses the music that is played on the radio?

10 Do any advertisers have any influence on us? Do they make us like or buy certain products?

11 Are the police realistic characters in this play?

12 What do Ross's last two speeches show?

Projects

1   Write alternative dialogues for the police station scenes. They might be conversations between, say, yourself and a friend when you have the radio on in the background or they might perhaps be conversations in the home of Ross's girlfriend and her parents. They disapprove of Ross who they say is 'always fooling around . . . should get a proper job'.

2   Suppose Ronny had not kept silent on his second appearance before the magistrates and the case had lasted longer. Improvise the scene. There is a 'bench' of three magistrates, the police will each give evidence, Ronny will be asked to give his side of the story. . . .

    What will the magistrates recommend should happen to Ronny?

3   Write the local newspaper's report of the events covered by the play. (In a previous edition, the paper has already reported on Ronny's first break-in and court appearance.)

4   Choose six records you like. Write, then tape 'links' to play between the records to show how you would present them 'on air' in your own radio show.

5   Write an imaginary (but convincing) story about a character who goes berserk in a busy supermarket, as a protest. Find a way of making it clear what the person's protest is about. (Junk food? High prices? Being unemployed and very hard-up? Being sacked – fairly or unfairly?) What other characters will be in your story? How will they react during the event and after the main character has been taken away or has escaped? (Think carefully about what is the most realistic ending.)

Language work

1 Do you think a regional accent is a handicap or something of which to be proud? Which accents do you like? What is the difference between an accent and a dialect? Various small, humorous booklets have been published which are supposed to be 'guides' to the various dialects. There is, for example, a booklet called *Cockney Rhyming Slang* and another called *Larn Yersel' Geordie.* There is also a *Lern Yerself Scouse* which contains 'translations' of Scouse nicknames and phrases such as 'gisalite' (Could you oblige me with a match, please?), 'de Mersey Funnel' (the Roman Catholic Cathedral of Liverpool) and 'Send im across de park!' (He is not good enough for our team but may be acceptable to Everton – or Liverpool, depending on who is speaking).

   Try compiling a guide to your regional (or school) dialect. Think how you will indicate the sounds of your accent.

2 Liverpool is famous for its jokes. You heard about the lion that escaped from the Liverpool safari park? The kids ate it.

   Try compiling your own anthology of local jokes. Do any (or indeed all of them) perpetuate 'stereo-types'? Are such jokes harmful in any way?

General

1 What can be included in a radio or television play that cannot be included in a stage play? (For example, a car chase.)

2 What can be included in a radio play that cannot be included in a television play?

3   Look at copies of *TV Times* and *Radio Times* and list
    Drama and Comedy series, serials and single plays.
    Which do the television companies show most of?
    Can you suggest reasons why they choose to show
    series and serials?

4   Some newspapers 'preview' forthcoming programmes.
    With the help of *Radio Times* and *TV Times*, try
    writing your own critical preview of some forthcom-
    ing programmes, making your own judgements on
    whether you would recommend them to other view-
    ers.

5   Do you like a play to be realistic? Which of the plays
    in this book do you find most convincing? Which do
    you like best? Why?

6   Do you prefer television plays that include a lot of
    location filming? Why or why not?

7   What weak points do some television plays have, so
    far as you are concerned?

8   Collect together a number of television reviews from
    various daily papers. Which do you think are fair?
    Try reviewing a programme you have seen recently
    (or one of the plays in this book).